"What a valuable treasure chest of insights into the mind of a teenage girl! This carefully crafted book is a must-read for any mom who desires to see her relationship with her teenage daughter move past the volley of words that pass between them and move into a new season where they can be joined at the heart. Thank you, Melody, for this superb handbook that gives us a glimpse into the teenage mind and equips us with understanding."

—ROBIN JONES GUNN, best-selling author of the
Christy Miller series and the Sisterchicks novels

"You think this is a book? It's really a bridge—no, a cord!—that will connect moms and daughters in a way to get through those turbulent teen years. Read it and reap!"

—DR. KEVIN LEMAN, best-selling author of *Have a New
Kid by Friday* and *Running the Rapids*

"When it comes to mom-daughter relationships, Melody Carlson gets it. In fact, I think Melody must have had our house bugged. She understands and she cares. *Dear Mom* is honest, authentic, practical, and hopeful."

—JIM BURNS, PHD, author of *Confident Parenting,
Teaching Your Children Healthy Sexuality,* and *Creating
an Intimate Marriage*

"Ever want to be let in on the running commentary going on inside your daughter's head? Now you can. With wit and honesty, Melody Carlson explains what every mom needs to know."

—REBECCA ST. JAMES, author, singer, and actress

EVERYTHING YOUR TEENAGE DAUGHTER WANTS
YOU TO KNOW BUT WILL NEVER TELL YOU

DEAR MOM

MELODY CARLSON

WATERBROOK
PRESS

Dear Mom
Published by WaterBrook Press
12265 Oracle Boulevard, Suite 200
Colorado Springs, Colorado 80921

ISBN 978-1-4000-7491-4
ISBN 978-0-30744-661-9 (electronic)

Published in the United States by WaterBrook Multnomah, an imprint of The
Doubleday Publishing Group, a division of Random House Inc., New York.

WATERBROOK and its deer colophon are registered trademarks of Random House Inc.

Library of Congress Cataloging-in-Publication Data
Carlson, Melody.
    Dear mom : everything your teenage daughter wants you to know but will never
tell you / Melody Carlson. — 1st ed.
        p. cm.
    ISBN 978-1-4000-7491-4 — ISBN 978-0-30744-661-9 (electronic)
    1. Teenage girls—Psychology. 2. Mothers and daughters—Psychology. I. Title.
    HQ798.C2742 2009
    649'.125—dc22

                                    2008049855

Printed in the United States of America
2009—First Edition

10 9 8 7 6 5 4 3 2 1

SPECIAL SALES
Most WaterBrook Multnomah books are available in special quantity discounts when
purchased in bulk by corporations, organizations, and special-interest groups. Custom
imprinting or excerpting can also be done to fit special needs. For information, please
e-mail SpecialMarkets@WaterBrookMultnomah.com or call 1-800-603-7051.

CONTENTS

WHY I WROTE THIS BOOK

A NOTE FROM THE AUTHOR

DEAR MOM,

Right up front, I want you to know that I do not consider myself an expert on parenting. Not at all! And I think parenting teenagers is the hardest job on the planet. I am so very thankful to have that behind me now (my sons are in their late twenties—a whole different kind of challenge). But for whatever reason, I seem to have an internal teen connection, understanding, empathy…whatever you want to call it. Or so my teen readers tell me in letters, e-mails, and book reviews.

In fact, one teen girl said to me, "Mrs. Carlson, I think you have a teenage girl trapped inside, uh, well"—she stammered for the right words—"inside the body of a middle-aged woman." Her cheeks turned red, and I had to laugh at the compliment (or was it an insult?).

She nailed it. I do have a teenage girl stuck inside me. The truth is, I do remember how it felt to be a teen, and I do relate to teenage challenges and struggles. That's why I write so many books for young adults. I have great empathy for teen girls, especially these days, when the world and stresses and pressures push in from all sides.

I also have empathy for moms, and I realize that it's easy to forget what it felt like to be a teen when you are trying to be the parent of a teen. Teens challenge us at every turn, and we want to come across as having it together and being intelligent and, you know, *the adult*. Because we're the grownups, we think we should have the answers and our kids should listen to us, and we even think we deserve a little respect from time to time.

Well, *think again.*

At least that's probably what your teen would say—and that's why I wrote this book. I want to help you understand, and maybe even remember, what it's like to be a teen. I want to help translate all those times your daughter comes into the kitchen and starts ragging on you for looking like Mrs. Frumpty-Dumpty, saying things like: "Get a clue, Mom, those Crocs are like so last year." What she's really saying is, "I'm hurt and angry today because my supposedly best friend made fun of me in front of a guy I like."

Of course, your daughter will never tell you that verbatim.

So take off your "parent" hat, consider wrapping the cover of this book in a brown paper bag (so the kids don't see you reading it), and see if some of the stuff in here doesn't help you make a little more sense of your girl and your lives together. Consider this your chance to walk a mile in your daughter's flip-flops.

Melody Carlson

WHY YOU SHOULDN'T READ THIS BOOK

A NOTE FROM YOUR DAUGHTER

DEAR MOM,

Maybe it's already too late to tell you to put down this book, because I know you don't like to waste your money. At least you don't like *me* to waste your money. Anyway, I know you want me to believe that you would never intentionally waste your money—not that I'm totally convinced of this, but never mind about me. It might not be too late for you, Mom. If you're still in the bookstore, trying to decide whether or not you'll like this book, wondering if it will be worth your time (oh, did I mention your money?), it's not too late to just set it down and walk away. Just walk away, and no one will get hurt, because, seriously, what is there about parenting me (your sweet, innocent teenage daughter) that you don't already get?

You're a cool mom—you can handle this, right?

Even if someone gave you this book, that doesn't mean you need to read it. Who cares if Grandma or Aunt Sue thought it was just the ticket to help you work out things with your beastly teenage daughter. We know Grandma and Aunt Sue aren't that smart about this stuff.

Oh, maybe they've heard you complain about me, or maybe they even heard me mouth off to you (that one time) or saw me freeze you out (I was irritated, okay?), so they decided you need this how-to book to straighten me out. Well, you know as well as I do that they just need to get a life. They obviously don't realize that you really do know what you're doing, Mom. They just can't appreciate that you already have things under control (everything but me, that is, and we both know that's not gonna happen). So why waste your time with this book?

You're still reading, aren't you? You're still not convinced? Fine, Mom, I'll make it easy for you. Here are six reasons why you should toss this book right now.

1. You won't like what you read, and you know the saying— ignorance is bliss.
2. You think you already know what's up with me. Why trust someone else to fill your head with nonsense?
3. You already know how to fix what you think is wrong with me.
4. Maybe you think I'm perfect as is... At least that's what I'm hoping.
5. Get real! You don't really have time for this. What mom does these days?
6. And finally, whatever happened to just leaving well enough alone? Things eventually work out, don't they?

I see you haven't given up yet. You're still reading. Well, don't say you weren't warned, and don't think that just because you're reading this book, written by a so-called teenage girl, that you're reading about me. I am a one-of-a-kind book and cannot be read or understood in a single volume.

ONE

THINGS I DON'T LIKE

ABOUT ME

I know you watch me sometimes, especially if you think I'm not looking. You might assume you're seeing who I really am. Maybe you are, but maybe you're not, because I have learned to hide certain things, especially those things I don't like about myself.

It's not easy to admit this, but I am practicing the art of concealment. I'm learning to disguise, even camouflage, the parts of me that don't measure up. You may ask what measuring device I'm using. Well, that just depends. It's all related to how I'm feeling at any given moment—and my feelings are constantly changing, and so is the specific insecurity I'm attempting to hide. Trust me, Mom, there are plenty of them.

The Interior Things

First, there are the inner things, those qualities that the adults in my life try to convince me are the most important, like being honest or kind or generous or faithful. I'm not saying those traits aren't important because, *duh,* I know they are, but it's difficult to get a grasp on them. It's like they turn into a slimy wet bar of soap that slips out of my hands.

For instance, I'm really trying to be honest and forthright and suddenly someone (maybe even you, Mom) asks me a tough question that I can't truthfully answer. Whether it's incriminating to me or you or someone else, I just cannot force myself to tell the truth. So I don't. Then I feel guilty. I dislike myself even more. Would I admit that to anyone? to you? I don't think so.

Or say I'm striving to be kinder to those around me. I know it's the right way to be, so I'm thinking kind thoughts and asking God to help me change this area of my life. Suddenly my younger sister, without even asking, borrows my favorite Lucky jeans and returns them ripped and dirty and buried in the bottom of my dirty-clothes hamper.

Well, kindness goes right out the window. Can you blame me? Yes, as a matter of fact, you can blame me, and you do. After baby sister runs crying to you, saying that I just called her mean names and threatened her life (which may or may not be true), you side with her. You put on your stern face and point out that I'm being selfish and mean, which really aggravates me.

I cannot help defending myself, which only makes me look worse. Okay, it makes me look *way* worse. My voice gets loud, and my anger flares. Will I back down? Will I admit that maybe I've been a bit harsh or a little cruel or even slightly vicious to baby sister? Will I apologize right then and there? Probably not, but maybe I'm thinking about it. Maybe I even want to bury the hatchet, but not when you're forcing me, Mom. Not if you're scowling and shaking your finger at me.

If and when I apologize, I want it to be on my terms, in my timing, and I'd prefer it to be somewhat sincere. Anything else and you're making me feel like a child. Okay, maybe I'm acting like a child, but give me a break, I'm trying to grow up. It's just not easy. I want to do one thing, but I end up doing another. I want to be one way, but I am totally the opposite.

I Am a Puzzle

Perhaps you're beginning to see a pattern in my life about now, or so you imagine, because it's a random pattern that cannot be predicted. It's a pattern of inconsistency and contradiction. You look at me and scratch your head as you wonder where you went wrong. You thought you were doing a good job. You assumed that you raised me to be such a nice girl, and you can't understand how I can be such a total monster at times. Then, just when you're ready to completely give up on me, I surprise you and do something genuinely nice.

Okay, I'll admit it. I'm a dichotomy, a mystery, a quandary (yes, I know some big words, but I don't use them much since I wouldn't want you to get the idea that I'm overly smart or you might complain about things like academic underachievement). The fact is, *I* don't even understand who I am. I often feel confused and frustrated. Just like you, I get disappointed in me. Not that I let it show—not intentionally, that is. Remember, that's the big cover-up.

So here's my confession, Mom: in the same way that I use a flesh-tone cosmetic concealer to hide a loathsome zit, I'm developing concealers to hide the things I don't want others to notice. It's just the game we girls play, Mom. For the most part, it's a game that most of us learn from our mothers.

Before you get all defensive, be honest with yourself, Mom. You were a teenager once too. You went through these very same things (maybe you're still going through them). You found yourself falling short in some areas and didn't always like who you were, but you devised ways to hide your insecurities. You had cover-ups for your weaknesses too.

Only now you're a grownup, and you pretend that you've got it all together, that you never fail, that you don't remember what it was like to be a struggling teen, or that you're not still concealing parts of yourself that you're not proud of. Maybe we're more alike than you think. Are you willing to admit that? to yourself? to your best friend? to me? You see, we women really are complicated, aren't we?

Those Outer Things

Trust me, Mom, it's not those important inner qualities that concern me the most. I started there, because I wanted to get your attention. I wanted to put my best foot forward and act like I'm deep and caring and want to be beautiful on the inside. I really do, but if the whole truth and nothing but the truth was revealed (and isn't that what I'm doing here?), I'm way more concerned about my exterior than my interior. Okay, it's kind of painful to admit that. It makes me sound shallow and superficial and insecure and sort of pathetic, but it's the truth.

As you like to point out (and I vehemently deny), I *am* influenced by what I see, whether it's movies, TV, magazines, MySpace, or whatever. I'm not blind. I can't help but notice the discrepancies in the way we look, and it seems to me we are not all created equal. Though I'd never say something this lame, I wouldn't complain if I woke up tomorrow looking like Jessica Alba.

Just for the record, Mom, I'm not stupid, and I don't live under a rock. I know I'm being duped by the media, but sometimes I just can't help it. Yeah, I'm fully aware that those glossy images are the result of painstaking hours of makeup and hairstyling by crafty professionals, who are paid big bucks to make ordinary women look absolutely fantastic. I know that models' photos are airbrushed and digitally tweaked to portray a picture of perfection. Yes, I know this in my head, but sometimes I don't believe it. Sometimes, like when I'm feeling particularly low, I am convinced that 99 percent of the females on this planet are prettier, skinnier, or just plain happier than I am. Some of them are all three. That is so unfair.

"You're such a pretty girl," you might say to me, as you catch me looking in the mirror and frowning. I can tell by the tone of your voice that you're feeling slightly sorry for me. You think this is what I need to hear.

"Yeah, right," I might say. You probably don't see me roll my eyes.

"Oh, you are, sweetie. *Everyone* says so."

"Everyone who?" Okay, now you've slightly piqued my interest. Do you mean *everyone* as in Josh Green, the hottie who lives across the street?

"Well…your grandmother was just saying—"

And that's when you lose me, Mom. Not that I think you're lying exactly, but you *are* my mother. What else are you going to tell me? What else would my grandmother say? Of course, you must think I'm pretty or at least act like it. I know that. It's your maternal, biological duty. The fact is, it just doesn't help.

When I look at myself, all I see are my imperfections. I try not to compare myself to others, but I can't help it. Maybe I learned that from you, back when I was a little girl and you didn't know I was watching you stand in front of the mirror, poking at your midsection or frowning at your nose or complaining about your hair. Maybe I'm just caught up in the female curse of our beauty-trap society of tummy tucks, Botox injections, liposuction, nose jobs, teeth whitening, breast implants, and breast reductions. We live in a never-good-enough culture. When I look at myself in the mirror, I think there is lots of room for improvement.

My Attempts at Improvements

So perhaps I decide to take matters into my own hands. I decide that, okay, I can't afford plastic surgery (not that you would ever let me, anyway), but I can work out more often. Maybe I can eat fewer french fries and drink more water. (Who knows? It might even help my complexion.)

I know you're freaking that I might become anorexic. (Okay, maybe I've toyed with the idea. What teen girl hasn't?) But commanding me to put an end to my self-improvement plan is not helping one bit. If anything, you make me want to dig in my heels and really go for it. (I really do like pizza, though.)

Seriously, Mom, the harder you push one way, the harder I will push the other way. So maybe you need to just trust me a little. Give me credit for having a little common sense. (Okay, maybe not consistently, but I'm not a total nut case either.) Give me a little space and see what I do. Better yet, maybe you can partner with me for a healthier lifestyle. I realize that you may know more than I do about

WAYS TO HELP MY SELF-ESTEEM

* Don't point out my flaws in public or in private.
* Be honest with me about your own self-esteem issues.
* Don't compare me to others.
* Show me that you love and accept me just as I am.
* Notice my achievements. Just don't throw a party.
* Don't make fun of my attempts to improve myself.
* Don't be too focused on outward appearances.
* Speak positively about my future.
* Don't dwell on my failures.
* Don't be too quick to help me.
* Don't pick on my wardrobe choices.
* Don't be overly sympathetic or coddling.
* Expect the best from me, but don't complain when I don't deliver.
* Don't belittle me or make me feel more like a child than I am.

foods that are good for us (like fruits and vegetables, whole grains, and good proteins). Maybe we can do this together, but instead of assuming the worst and pushing the panic button, give me a chance to figure out some things for myself.

Yes, I know you hear frightening reports about girls my age with eating disorders. Trust me: I know it's a real thing. I have eyes. I have friends. I see what goes on. Okay, if I show signs of anorexia or bulimia, you should be concerned. Hopefully, you would be honest but gentle with me, and we would work together to deal with it. But you should know that I need to feel I have some control in my life. I need to grow up; just don't *tell* me I need to grow up. That will only bring out the immature side of me.

I've barely scratched the surface of the things I don't like about myself. It would be embarrassing to list all of them, but I can give you a generic list, a list I've compiled based on my friends' comments. The list starts with, "I hate my hair. It's too curly, too straight, too thin, too thick." It moves on to, "I hate my eyes. They're too small, too big, too blue, too close together, too far apart." Then it goes on to, "I hate my nose. It's too fat, too skinny, too long, too short." Then it's, "I hate my zits," "I hate my freckles," "I hate my ears," and, "I need lip injections," or, "I need a boob job," "My feet are too big," "My thighs are too fat," and, "My butt's too small." You get the picture. I'm sure you can guess at other things on my list, even if I don't mention them here.

I wonder if you remember how you felt when you were my age. Do you recall the things you didn't like about yourself, way back in the Dark Ages? I'll bet your list wasn't all that different from mine.

Or maybe you were perfect and you have no complaints about adolescence. In that case, don't talk to me.

Taking Off Masks

Here's the thing, Mom: it would probably help me if you were willing to admit some of the things you struggled with as a teen. If you could get real and tell me about some of your own challenges with self-esteem, identity issues, self-image, or even some of the things that still bother you as an adult, who knows, if you get transparent with me, I might be willing to let my guard down a bit more around you. Okay, no promises here, but it could happen.

I should warn you that *timing is everything,* my timing, that is. Just because you might suddenly get the urge to disclose your deepest, darkest secrets (as you're driving me to school one morning), does *not* mean I'm ready to hear about it at that particular moment. I mean, I might be so busy obsessing over my own life and troubles or freaking over whether or not my hair looks okay or if Jeremy is going to talk to me in geometry today that I could really care less about your past.

Sorry. It may sound shallow and selfish, but it's the truth. Still, if you catch me at the right time—and I'll try to give you some clues—it could be life changing. Or at least it might bring us a little closer, until I need my space anyway and have to remind you to back off again. Maybe I'll remind you a bit more gently next time. Who knows?

TWO

THINGS I DON'T LIKE

ABOUT YOU

race yourself. First of all, I do love you, Mom. I probably don't say it enough, and I'm sure I don't act like it most of the time, but I do love you, and I hope you'll always know that. Second, there are some things I don't like about you. Oddly enough, some of them are the very same things that I used to love about you when I was younger. I wonder which one of us changed.

For instance, I used to love it when you helped me with clothes and hair and all that girl stuff. I loved that kind of attention and thought you had pretty good taste back then, but I was just a little girl, and hey, what did I know? Besides, you seemed to be enjoying yourself. I mean, you got to have your fun, even if it was short-lived.

When I was little, you made most of the decisions about the clothes I'd wear or how I'd wear my hair that day. I just agreed, most of the time anyway, and you seemed proud of me when we were out and about. But was that really me, Mom? Or was I simply playing a miniature you? Okay, don't get mad. I'm just being truthful. You like honesty, right?

It's My Life

Do you want to know what really ticks me off, now that I'm not a little girl anymore? Sometimes you still act like you should have the final say on my appearance. Like maybe you think I'm your own personal property. Seriously, Mom, sometimes it feels like you think you're responsible for every move I make and even the air I breathe. It can feel stifling. It's like you think I'm this extension of you, and if I go out of the house wearing an outfit you don't approve of, you totally freak. You act like my choice in clothing is a slap in the face. I just don't get that.

I am not you, Mom. Maybe that's the whole point of some of my choices in attire. I want you to understand that I'm my own person now and I don't want to be you. *I want to be me.* Is that so wrong? Do you have any idea how you make me feel when you give me that look of disapproval, disdain, and (sometimes) disgust? How would you like it if someone treated you like that or looked at you like that?

Sometimes it feels like you're embarrassed to be with me. Oh, you might not say as much, but I can feel it, and it hurts. It's like you can't handle the fact that I look like me, instead of looking like a miniature you. I'm sure you're worried that one of your friends will see me and think I'm a poor reflection on you, like someone is going to judge your mothering abilities based on my personal style. But is it possible that you're taking yourself too seriously?

When you were my age, did your mother approve of your appearance 24/7? I don't think so, but maybe I should talk to Grandma about this. I'm sure she'd have something to say.

Instead of worrying about my clothes, why not lighten up a little? Or, like I've heard some grownups say, maybe you should pick your battles more carefully. Like what if I started drinking or doing drugs? Wouldn't the whole fashion issue suddenly seem a little silly?

Give Me Space

Keep in mind, Mom, that in this adolescent search for myself, I might have a little technical difficulty from time to time. I mean, this whole dance is not easy for me. It's not like I've been a teen for that long, and it's not like they teach you this stuff in school. Do you have any idea how much fashion criticism (beyond yours) I face on a regular basis? At least I'm trying, and I'm hoping to improve with age. Couldn't you just be a bit more patient until I get there?

I mean, unless I go out looking like a skanky hooker, or I tattoo or pierce my body parts (which I do not think will happen), why not give me some space? As hard as it is to accept, I am not your little girl anymore. In case you haven't noticed, I've grown, and you can't hold me down and dress me in pink ruffles or preppy polo shirts if I don't cooperate. The sooner you get this, the happier we'll both be. In fact, the whole planet might sigh in relief.

You're Not My Friend

Here's another heads-up, Mom—something else I'm not fond of. Sorry to be so blunt, but you kind of asked for it by buying this book and reading this far, although I have to give you credit for sticking it out. Okay, I'll admit there was a time when I thought it was fun for you to hang with my friends and me. Sometimes we even treated you like you were one of us. That was kind of cool, but the cool factor wore off as I got older.

Just because you're my mom does not mean you're one of my friends. Sure, you might occasionally get lucky. If we're feeling congenial and decide to let you in on something, we might even laugh at one of your corny jokes, but this cannot happen on a regular basis. My friends are my turf, and I need you to respect that. I also need you to keep some things private—specifically, the embarrassing kinds of things you happen to know about me. While we're at it, you can also keep some of those embarrassing things about our family quiet too. Mum's the word, Mom.

A really important tip, Mom: if you say something about me—something that makes my friends laugh at me—it is so *not* funny. You need to get that. The time might come when these things change, or my skin gets thicker (and, hopefully, less zitty), but trust me, change will come a lot sooner if you take my advice now. Mothers should not make fun of their daughters while friends are watching.

Act Your Age

There's something else you might not be aware of, Mom. Uh, you're not a teenager anymore. I know I've been trying to remind you of how you felt when you were my age, but it's not like I want you to live there permanently. What I'm saying is, please don't pretend you're a teenager. I mean, sure, you can dress cool (well, not too cool), and you can change your hairstyle, but don't forget that you are my mom. I appreciate it when you act like a responsible grownup, even if I forget to tell you so. Even when I act aggravated because you remind me that you *are* the mom, I'm secretly relieved. I know, I probably sound all confusing and contradictory again, but remember what I said about inconsistency. It's the way my life seems to run. Hopefully, it won't always be like this.

There's just a certain security in knowing that your parents are your parents, not your buddies. I mean, I already have friends, and when my friends observe someone's mom acting like she thinks she's sixteen, well, trust me, it can get pretty ugly. Oh, sure, they won't say these things to her face, but they will say them. The fact is, whether we show it or not, we respect you older folks a lot more when you act your age.

Speaking of acting your age, here's another thing I cannot stand. Okay, I know I'm a kid and I can act like a little snot sometimes, but it's infuriating when you drop down to my level and act like me. I know you're not perfect and only human, but here's another news flash, Mom: *you are the parent.* So even if I'm losing it and acting totally immature, it doesn't help when you act the same way. Not only do I lose respect for you, but it's totally uncool, and, to be perfectly frank, it shakes my world. Trust me, sometimes my world is already shaking pretty hard.

Anger Doesn't Work

We all lose our tempers occasionally, but take it from me, Mom, anger is a really bad parenting tool. For one thing, it's a horrible example. I mean, you sure don't like it when I lose my cool, so why would you want to lose yours in front of me? It makes you look smaller to me, and once again, I don't respect you as much. Beyond that, it totally distracts me from what's really going on at the moment.

If you start lambasting me for putting a dent in the car, I totally block out the fact that it happened while I was talking on my cell phone (and I know that's a big no-no). I get so hurt and mad when you're yelling at me that I don't admit to the real cause of the fender bender. In a way, your anger will prevent me from learning lessons I need to learn, like being honest and responsible.

When you lose your temper, you make it easy for me to blame you for everything, and in a way, I'm not wrong. In another way, I'm not right either. Mostly, I'm just confused and frustrated, so why not leave anger out of the parenting game?

I Need Consistency

I realize I've gone on and on about inconsistencies and contradictions, but I've been referring to my own mixed-up life. I can admit that I tend to swing back and forth; whether it's hormonal or just my rite of passage, I can't say for absolute sure, but I know I can be unpredictable and inconsistent. Even so, here's the thing, Mom, I don't want you to be like that too. I need you to be consistent and responsible and somewhat predictable. In some ways you are like my rock and one of the major stabilizing factors in my life. I need you to be my rock-solid mom.

If you give me your word on something, I need you to keep it. I want to depend on you to do what you say you'll do. I might be painting myself into a corner here, but I want you to be consistent in the ways you deal with me in regard to your rules and boundaries. I want your yes to mean yes and your no to mean no (for the most part anyway). I realize this whole thing could backfire on me. And for that reason, I'll attach a small disclaimer here. I know that sometimes it's impossible to be 100 percent consistent, because circumstances, people, and life can change, and I don't want you to be so locked into something that you turn into a tyrant. I just want to know that I can depend on you to parent me, without feeling like we're on a roller-coaster ride. I mean, hey, my life already has plenty of ups and downs. I don't want you to be one of them.

TEN WAYS TO HUMILIATE ME

1. Treat me like a baby or talk down to me in front of my friends.
2. Lose your temper in front of my friends.
3. Use a pet name in front of my friends.
4. Tell about an embarrassing moment in front of my friends.
5. Show up at my school dressed in something uncool.
6. Discipline me in front of my friends.
7. Try to act cool around my friends, like you're just one of the girls.
8. Show too much affection in public—to me or anyone else.
9. Don't take care of your own personal appearance.
10. Do drugs or overly indulge in alcohol or any other addictive behavior.

Don't Check Out on Me

I realize my next point could sound contradictory to what I've already declared about needing my space and autonomy, but, like I keep trying to say, I often feel like a walking, talking dichotomy. Everything in my life is split in half. It's a love-hate, hot-cold, good-bad, right-wrong sort of world I live in. I can't explain it except to say that someday I hope things will change, because I'd hate to think I'll always feel this mixed-up.

I heard a teacher jokingly say that adolescence is a form of temporary insanity. He told us that our brains are messed up right now. It has to do with hormones and brain development and all kinds of biochemical things, but he also said that by our midtwenties we should be functioning normally. So there's hope. Quite honestly, Mom, I sometimes *do* feel crazy. Like maybe someone should lock me up and hide the key for a few years. On the other hand, I might just be a teenager, trying to figure out her life.

So back to my point: although I hardly ever say this and it sounds like I'm backtracking, I really appreciate your being there for me. Despite all my talk about needing my freedom and independence, I really don't want it too soon or too completely. I don't want you to check out of my life. I need to know that you're here and that you still care, even when I don't show it.

I know kids with checked-out parents, and let me tell you, it looks like a pretty sad situation to me. Oh, the kids might act like it's no big deal. They may even brag about how they have so much freedom, but I can see the sadness in their eyes, and I can tell by their actions and choices that the lack of parenting in their lives is impacting them big time. Despite all my whining and complaining, I really don't want that.

I realize you have your own life, Mom. You're a busy woman with your own interests and responsibilities, but I really appreciate it when you're willing to set some of those things aside for me. I'm sure that sounds selfish and self-centered, but hey, it's the truth. Don't worry, it won't be long before I grow up and take off, and then you'll have plenty of time to do your own thing.

I might not show it, but most of the time I'm secretly glad when you pop in at some event I'm involved in. I'm actually impressed that you even remembered to come, because I know how hectic your schedule can be. So even if I act uncomfortable or embarrassed, I think it's pretty cool that you cared enough to make the effort to show up, just for me.

THREE

RELATIONSHIPS CONFUSE ME

SOMETIMES

So far, I've focused on my relationship with you, Mom, and as you know, that's hard on both of us. What you may not fully appreciate is that I have a lot of other relationships that can get almost as messed up. I don't like to let on that I sometimes feel relationally challenged. That sounds so lame, and it probably doesn't help when I see your relationships with your friends going so much more smoothly than my relationships with my friends, though I suppose that gives me a smidgen of hope. Maybe someday I'll figure it out.

In the meantime, here are a few things you should know about me and certain relationships.

It's not always easy to hang with other teenage girls who have as many ups and downs and problems as I have. Oh, sure, if we're commiserating together, complaining about lame parents or Nazi teachers or some dumb boy who can't keep his hands to himself, everything's cool. But occasionally a "friend" will turn on me. For no rational reason whatsoever, someone I thought I could trust will rip the floor right out from under me and even embarrass me in public. That can really hurt. When this happens, do I run home and tell Mommy about it? Do I whine and cry on your shoulder? No way. I gave that up in middle school.

Besides wanting to avoid the humiliation of admitting I'm a

failure within my circle of friends, I know that you just wouldn't get it. I'm sorry, Mom, but it's true. You'd probably say something like, "Oh, don't let it get to you. You've got lots of other nice friends." But that's not the problem. The problem is that I'm feeling bummed because of how a certain girl treated me, and whether or not it makes sense to you, I might still want her to be my friend. Or I might simply want to kill her. However, neither scenario would be acceptable to you, so I keep my mouth shut. Do you know what happens then?

Because I'm feeling bad about what occurred that day—a painful incident that I don't intend to disclose to a parent who probably wouldn't get it—I am accused of being moody, like I'm choosing to feel bad. The truth is, I'm simply feeling hurt and confused. Okay, now I can hear you. You're wondering why I don't just come out and tell you about it. You're thinking that you would understand, that you would make me feel better. Okay, I'll remind you of something that happened a few years ago.

Maybe You Don't Always Know Best

It went something like this: "What's wrong, sweetie?" I'm thirteen and sitting in the passenger seat while you drive me home from school. I'm feeling seriously bummed because my best friend, Ashley Peterson, said something mean to me at lunch. So I tell you, "Nothing's wrong." I'm already preparing to push you away from me.

"Come on," you urge. "You can tell me."

I fall into your trap. "Okay," I begin slowly. "Ashley said something mean to me today."

"What did she say?"

"She told me that I shouldn't be eating french fries for lunch."

"Oh?" Okay, you almost look like you're going to laugh, and I begin to feel offended and defensive.

"It's not funny, Mom. Right there in front of God and everyone, Ashley told me that eating french fries was the reason I've been gaining weight."

Now you glance at me as if you might agree with Ashley (and I want to scream), but you just nod like you feel sympathetic and, once again like an adolescent fool, I fall for it.

"See, Mom," I say, continuing to lay my cards on the table, "just a couple of days ago, I confessed to Ashley how much I weigh. I told her the real number, then swore her to secrecy. And right there in front of all our friends, she announced how much I weigh."

Now you frown. "Well, that really was mean."

I nod. "I know."

"Well, that Ashley," you say with a slightly disgusted tone you probably think is going to make me feel better. "She has always had a mean side, sweetie. I've tried to tell you that. So maybe it's just as well. There are lots of other nice girls who could..." And you ramble on and on, naming names of girls who would be good best friends and yada-yada-blah-blah-blah, and I tune you right out.

So here is the deal, Mom: I still wanted Ashley to be my best friend. I wanted her to say she was sorry, maybe even publicly. That night she called me and sweetly apologized, but you continued to act like Ashley was bad news. I know you wanted me to find another best friend, and, okay, maybe you were right, since Ashley eventually hurt me and dumped me. But that's another story. Do you see what I'm trying to say here? You don't always know what's best, or maybe it's just that your timing is off.

Sisterly Love

Speaking of relationships, it's not exactly easy being a sister, Mom. As much as you want me to love my siblings and be kind to them, you sure go about it all wrong. "How's that?" you ask innocently. Well, you often take their word over mine. Why is that? Is it because one is younger or because another is your beloved son? Is it because you believe the lies my sister tells about me? Is it because you love my brother more? What?

Seriously, Mom, sometimes it feels like you favor the other one. Of course, you will deny this. You go out of your way to say you love your children equally. But that's not always how you act. Sometimes you put more pressure on me than someone else. You say it's because I'm your daughter and you expect more of me. How fair is that? How is that going to help me love my sibling more? Maybe you should think about that.

I know I'm not exactly easy and my teen years are probably wearing you out, but just you wait, Mom, baby sister won't be easy either. I mean, she's only a few years behind me. Just think of all the fun you might have with her down the line. Or how you'll feel when your beloved son casts you aside for, say, football. So why don't you try treating your kids more like equals? Who knows, it might improve things. Just for the record, Mom, I don't really hate my sibs. I just like to say that to let off steam. Here's another news flash: when I say I hate my sis or my bro, or even if I say I hate you, I'm usually thinking that I hate myself. Am I going to say that? I don't think so.

Best Worst Friends

Back to the subject of friends—yes, you were right about Ashley (although it took a few years before I figured it out). What you probably don't realize is that, after being hurt by her, I am cautious with my new best friend. In fact, I'm not even sure Madison really is my best friend. I'm not even sure I know what a best friend is supposed to look like anymore. At the same time, I don't want to be without one. That would be pathetic, so I put up with some things.

Do I tell you about these things? Of course not! I can only imagine what you would say if I told you. You might even ban Madison from our house. So I keep my mouth shut. Her family has problems, and I suppose she's going through even more rebellion than I am, but I see her side of things. You might not get this, but I am trying to love her the way God loves us—unconditionally. But I have a feeling that if you knew more about her (okay, she drinks sometimes, and I saw her smoke one of her stepdad's cigars, and she occasionally uses colorful language), the unconditional-love thing would be tossed right out the window, so I don't tell you everything.

I'm not stupid, Mom. I can see when Madison is blowing it, and sometimes I even point this out to her. That may eventually be the undoing of our friendship. Still, it's my friendship (not yours), and if I want to blow it up, that's my choice. If I stick around, that's my choice too. Just because I'm her friend does not mean I will drink or smoke cigars or swear. Of course, it doesn't mean that I won't, either. I guess only time will tell.

Mean Girls

Here's another thing I probably won't talk to you about. I know I *used* to, back in middle school, and you were actually sympathetic, albeit somewhat misinformed. You told me there probably wouldn't be mean girls in high school. You thought they'd outgrow it. Think again, Mom. Their tactics might've changed, but they're still around. Mostly I try to ignore them or act like their comments, looks, and snipes don't hurt. Of course, they do hurt, and sometimes I wonder why some people have to be so mean.

I know what you'd say, because you've said it before, but I'm not sure I agree or that I really care. I know you think the reason they're mean is because something is making them deeply unhappy. That might be true, but some of them seem to be mean just because they want to be mean. Period.

I confess: sometimes I do the same thing. Sometimes, for no good reason, I am mean. (There, I've said it. Don't ever expect me to say it out loud.) Then, after I'm done being mean (usually to you or to baby sister or occasionally to a friend who is aggravating me), I feel bad and I feel guilty and I feel like I am a really poor excuse for a Christian and I hope it will be the last time I ever do something mean. Then I wonder, *Will there ever be a last time?* I'm not sure how you'd answer that one, Mom, and let's be honest here, I've seen you be mean too. Sometimes it's very subtle (and you might not even realize I'm watching), but it makes me sad.

Ex-Friends

Here's another confession: I feel guilty over friends I've left behind, friends I dumped for selfish reasons. Of course, I'm not going to admit this to you, Mom. It sounds mean and unloving and unkind— all those things I'm not supposed to be. But I didn't know what else to do. In some ways, I felt I was running for my life. I know it was wrong, but how do you undo something like that?

For instance, when I see Jessica Burns, I feel torn. You remember Jessica. I dumped her at the beginning of my sophomore year. On one hand, she was a loyal friend, and she liked going to youth group and took her faith seriously. On the other hand, she was totally boring and liked to obsess over dumb things. So what was I supposed to do? If I hung with her, I would be classified as being just as lame as she was. Like I said, I ran for my life. I started hanging with Madison and her friends, and we have fun. Okay, sometimes it's not completely fun, and sometimes some of my friends aren't very nice, but sometimes they are. Besides, don't forget I've been dumped by a best friend too. Maybe it's just one of those things—what goes around comes around.

The problem is, when I see Jessica, she gives me that sad-eyed look, and I feel totally guilty and like the lowest lowlife on the planet. Do I do anything about it? No way. I walk right by, pretending I don't see her. That's when I know I'm acting like a mean girl. I don't usually think of myself as a mean girl, not like some of them anyway. I wonder if I'll ever figure this one out.

Still, I don't want you to lecture me on this, Mom. Okay, maybe just a gentle word of advice, if you don't drone on and on, might come in handy. Or maybe it wouldn't. Who can tell?

So are you starting to see that my life isn't as simple and fun and carefree as you like to believe? Are you feeling a tiny speck of empathy for me and girls like me, who are trying to find our way through this complicated, confusing, contradictory adolescent world, without being completely destroyed along the way?

The Stickiest Relationships

This is a tough one, Mom, and a subject I will always try to avoid with you, because I know where it will end up. Oh, I might pretend to discuss boys, or even a certain guy, but it's probably just to throw you off my trail.

Here's the problem: I always seem to like a guy who doesn't like me back. Although I keep this top secret, it plays havoc with my self-image. I mean, why does he not like me back? Why does he go out with a girl who has zero personality and isn't even that cute? Why? Why? Why? Don't answer. I know you'd probably say something like, "He's still young. He just doesn't know what a great girl you are." Or my all-time least favorite, "There are lots of fish in the sea." Give me a break! I'm casting my line for that particular fish, and I don't really care about any of the others.

So another guy might notice me, and I'll tell myself, *Hey, that guy's not half bad,* and maybe Madison will point out his good qualities. Then I go out with him, and I get to know him a little, and, well, he seems to have only one thing on his mind. I've heard Dad say that seventeen-year-old boys are running on pure testosterone and that it's just the way they are and they should be avoided at all cost. That's pretty harsh, and it's just not going to happen.

I've also heard you say, "Why don't you just be friends with

HOW TO ACT AROUND MY FRIENDS

* It's okay to get to know my friends. Just don't be too obvious.
* Try to remember their names, and don't call them by the wrong names.
* Make them feel welcome in our home.
* Be friendly but not intrusive.
* Never criticize my friends, even if they're not around to hear.
* Respect my choices in friends.
* Keep your opinions about my friends to yourself.
* Don't make assumptions about my friends. If you have genuine cause for concern, tell me — gently.
* Trust that I will figure out which girl is a good friend and which one is not.
* Remember that valuable lessons can be learned from mistakes.

*

so-and-so?" Seriously, Mom, do you know how difficult that is? Do you really think there are a lot of guys out there who want to just be friends? Okay, I'll admit it sounds kind of good sometimes, but it just ain't happening. At least, not yet. Maybe someday.

Maybe there's something wrong with me, but I do like the idea of a guy really liking me (I mean, if he's a cool guy), and I do like the idea of being treated special (unless he's just trying to get me into bed). Do I sound conflicted? Well, *duh*. It's like walking through a minefield to figure this one out. This is what you need to know, Mom: I do not need you to keep trying to explain the whole thing to me. Sure, it's nice that you care, but if you keep saying the same thing over and over and over, I just stop listening.

Why don't you wait for me to ask you about something before you start dumping? Then, if you're smart, you won't unload everything you know all at once, and maybe you can influence me by offering one single morsel of your vast wisdom. Maybe that will make me want to come back for more. Do you get that?

Here's what I think: I am not going to totally understand boys and dating and relationships for a long time. I mean, look at you and Dad. It's not like you've got this thing totally nailed either. Okay, you might be ahead of me in some areas—not all—but I think you've still got a few things to learn too.

Comparisons, Jealousy, and...Who Am I, Anyway?

As I've mentioned, there is a fair amount of competition within my circle of friends. Sometimes it's kind of fun, and sometimes it's exhausting. Sometimes I feel like I'm swimming against the tide and will never find my way to solid ground, but sometimes I'm riding a wave, and I feel on top of the world. Then I can get slammed down. Do you get what I'm saying?

Probably the hardest part of having friends is that we're always comparing ourselves to each other. Oh, we don't actually say the words—that would sound lame—but trust me, it happens. It's the never-ending game of who's on top. It could be who's wearing the coolest clothes...who has the cutest hair, the best body, the clearest complexion, the hottest boyfriend, the most money, you name it. Insinuations are tossed around, and a girl can't help but make comparisons. Though we try not to show it, I'm pretty sure these comparisons lead to jealousy and those old familiar feelings: I'm not good enough, pretty enough, or thin enough. The list goes on and on. Fortunately, we seem to take turns at being on top, and sometimes we even offer false flattery to soothe a wounded ego. Still, I'm sure it's not healthy.

Now you might think that because some of my friends are Christians and go to church, they would be exempt from this kind of childish behavior. Think again, Mom. This isn't something I will tell you, because I'm pretty sure it would launch a lecture I don't want to endure. All I'm saying is that it's rough out there, and sometimes you don't help.

Like when I want to buy a certain pair of shoes or jeans (okay, I know they aren't cheap), you go into this whole routine of, "Why are you buying that? Are you just trying to keep up with the Joneses?" It makes me want to scream. Naturally, I deny that I'm trying to keep up with anyone. I say, "I just like them because I like them!" Well, *duh,* that's not exactly the truth. I mean, I do like my Lucky jeans, but I probably wouldn't like them nearly as much if my friends weren't already wearing them.

I really wish I were more mature and confident and self-assured so that buying a certain item of clothing wasn't so essential, but the truth is, I'm not there yet. Does that mean I'm hopeless? I hope not. I think it just means I need more time, Mom.

FOUR

I NEED YOU

BUT YOU CAN'T MAKE ME ADMIT IT

Okay, I realize I've pretty much raked you over the coals by telling you all the stuff I don't like about you. That had to be rough. Maybe you need a little break, so in this chapter I'll try to say a few nice things. Forgive me if they come across wrong or negative. It's just that old adolescent charm leaking out again. Bear with me.

Here's the deal: I need you, Mom. As you can probably guess, it's unlikely that I'll ever admit to this statement in public—and never in front of my friends. The truth is, I might not even confess to it in private, unless I'm a lot older or someone is holding a gun to my head.

But, yes, it's true: I do need you, just not in the old ways I used to need you. As I've mentioned, I do not need you to pick out my clothes or to make suggestions about my hair or makeup. I do not need you to comment on my friends or to tell me to stand up straight. I do not need you to pretend to be my buddy or to snoop around in my room. But there are some very specific things I *do* need from you.

I Need You for Stability

I've already mentioned that you are a rock in my life, Mom. Okay, sometimes it feels like I'm caught between you and a hard place, and that's not so great. But a lot of the time, I feel much more secure just knowing you are who you are. I appreciate knowing that, even if you seem stodgy at times, you remain a stabilizing force in my life. Just in case I forget to tell you before I turn thirty, I am thankful for that.

Here's another confession: when I get hurt or scared, you're usually the first person who comes to mind. I want my mommy! I also remind myself to cry out for God at times like that, but part of me will still cry out for you to come to my rescue. However, let's get real. If I ever really did cry out for my mommy, I would be so embarrassed, and if you came running to my rescue while my friends were around, I would die of humiliation. So let's keep this just between us.

I Need You to Be Honest

I might throw a fit if you say, "I'm just being honest with you," after you've informed me that my eye makeup is too heavy, but I actually appreciate your honesty. Not so much as a personal critique, but I rely on you to play no tricks on me. I need that, especially when there are so many people in my life who don't speak the truth or may use the truth to beat me up.

It might not seem like I'm making much progress, but I hope to become more honest. It feels good to tell the truth, especially if I'm not hurting someone with it. Unfortunately, it's not always easy to tell the truth. Sometimes little white lies seem like an easy way out, but I know they can come back to bite you.

Anyway, thank you for being honest. Thank you for living your best life. You may never know how much I need that.

I Need You for Security

My security comes from knowing that you're not going anywhere, Mom. I see other parents splitting up and heading their separate ways, and I see how their kids suffer as a result. I really need you to stick around.

I remember the night I found out that my boyfriend, Blake, liked Amy McCall better than he liked me. I came home broken-hearted. Naturally, I didn't tell you. You said good night, walked down the hall, and closed your bedroom door, just as usual. It's hard to explain, but it was oddly reassuring to know that, although my world felt temporarily shaken, you were in your room, just a couple of doors down the hall from me. I knew that if I needed to talk, I could go to your room and talk to you. Even better, I knew you were there, right where you were supposed to be.

My friend Darcy makes jokes about how her mom (recently divorced) has turned into quite a party girl who often stays out late and forgets to call. Darcy acts like she thinks it's funny, but I can see that it bugs her. She has lost her security. Thanks for not being like that, Mom. I really do appreciate it. Despite my attempts to act grown-up and independent, I need that kind of security in my life.

I Need Your Humor

Okay, you're probably wondering about this one. It's not like I think your jokes are all that clever or funny—especially when my friends are around—but I really do appreciate your attempts at humor.

When life gets stressful and you're able to lighten up and not take things too seriously, it really helps me and everyone around me. Your humor defuses the situation, and we're able to regroup and move on.

Whether you notice or not, I often follow your lead. Naturally, it's not something I want to admit (I mean, that I learn a thing or two from you), but sometimes when I'm with my friends and things get a little messed up, I try to lighten the atmosphere with humor. Amazingly, it works sometimes.

I suppose it's a challenge to always have a sense of humor when you're parenting teens. I'm sure I can stretch you to the limit. Just know that your humor is a good thing. I need it, and I think you do too!

I Need You to Have Self-Control

It probably sounds a bit strange for me, Ms. Big Mouth, to tell you, Ms. Mature Mom, that I need you to have self-control. Where have I heard that line before? The fact of the matter is that I do. I realize you're not perfect and sometimes you lose it. Okay, to be fair, I sometimes aid and abet in the losing-it part. But it is so cool when you don't lose it, Mom. I can't help but be impressed when you exercise self-control, especially when my friends are around.

I don't think I've ever been prouder of you than the time when Madison and I came home a full hour after curfew. I hadn't called (I told you my cell phone was dead, but I'm sure you knew that I'd actually just forgotten), and I could tell that you were worried about the icy roads that night. I had warned Madison, who was spending the night at our house, that you might blow up over this minor indiscretion.

Not only did you keep your cool, but you didn't even discipline me in front of her. You simply pointed out that it was very late and that I hadn't called and that you'd been worried. Did you see my jaw drop when you calmly told me you'd talk to me about it in the morning? True to your word, we did talk about it, but not until Madison went home the next day. Okay, you grounded me for the following weekend, but all things considered, it could've been worse.

Sometimes I Need Your Advice

Okay, I realize this is a tricky one, and I'm skating on thin ice to even mention it. Here's the deal, Mom: I do need your advice, but I'll always receive it better if (1) I ask you, (2) we're having an open discussion (not a lecture!), or (3) I'm about to do something so stupid or dangerous that you can't help yourself.

Take it from me: giving advice to anyone is always risky. Sometimes when I offer advice to a friend, she comes back all defensive, and I have to take it back and pretend I didn't mean it. The thing about advice is that it can sound like criticism. No one needs much of that.

I learned something interesting the other day. I learned that if I pair a bit of advice with a compliment, it works way better than the advice alone. (Okay, maybe I learned that one from you.) During PE last week, we were playing soccer (Madison pretty much stinks at soccer). Anyway, I was getting all competitive and wanted our team to win, so I said to Madison, "Hey, you're getting really good at controlling the ball." She seemed pleased. I added, "Why don't you try passing a little more often?" Well, on the next play, she passed to me, and I scored a goal. Guess what? We won.

Maybe it's like that old *Mary Poppins* song. (Do you remember how you used to make us watch that movie, because it was your favorite?) Maybe Mary Poppins was talking about giving advice when she sang, "A spoonful of sugar helps the medicine go down."

I Always Need Your Respect

You always tell me, "Respect is a two-way street." Yes, I know this. I'll admit I'm not that good at giving respect to you, but maybe if you hit me with a little respect first, I would try harder. Or maybe not. I'm making no promises.

Just because I'm a teenager does not mean I don't need respect, Mom. In fact, I think teens need it more than anyone. Why? Because there is so much disrespect going on in our world, and sometimes we don't even respect ourselves. I think if we could get a little more respect at home, it might help to balance things out.

For instance, you've been nagging me to clean my room. You act like I don't care that it looks like a pigsty. But the truth is, I do. Am I going to admit that to you? I don't think so, but the more you bug me about cleaning it, the more I dig my heels in. I've told you several times that I will get to it when I have time. If you could just respect me and trust me to keep my word, I would probably get to it a whole lot sooner. Seriously, how do you like it when someone keeps telling you to do something you already plan to do? Doesn't it make you feel like that person thinks you're a child or irresponsible or just plain lazy? Do you feel motivated by someone who refuses to back off and continues to nag and pick on you? Well, I don't. It just makes me mad. Trust me, Mom, a little respect will get much better results.

Be Interested, but Not *Too* Interested

This is one of those complicated needs. I mean, a pinch of interest can go a long way. I do want you to show an interest in my life—my grades, my friends, my activities—just not too much interest. I guess you'll have to figure out how to balance that.

It feels good (for the most part) that you want to know where I am and what I'm doing and that I am okay, but I don't want you breathing down my neck or questioning me all the time. Even when I complain about it, it's actually reassuring that you know what classes I'm taking and how I'm doing in them. It's kind of an accountability factor for me. I just don't want you constantly nagging me.

As I've already mentioned, I don't mind that you know a few things about my friends, but don't get too nosy. Whatever you do, don't eavesdrop on our conversations when we think we're speaking privately.

Speaking of privacy, I'd like to think that my room is *my* room. I'd like to think that you respect my privacy, that you don't poke around when I'm not there, that you don't read my journal or sneak into my e-mail or go through my drawers unless I ever give you a reason to be concerned—which isn't in my plans. If you ever think I am doing something dangerous or illegal, I suppose the rules would change. Let's not go there. That would be a different book, probably written by Dr. Phil.

I've already said this, but you need to hear it again. I do need to depend on you—just not in visible or obvious ways. I need to know you'll be there for me when things get rough. Just don't overdo it.

I am trying to become more independent, to stand on my own two feet. Though I know I'm not ready to be totally on my own, I suppose I try to convince myself that I am ready. I try to act like I'm a grownup and can handle my life. I might even act slightly cocky at times. I know that irks you, but you shouldn't take me too seriously.

I still have a lot to learn, and if it's any comfort to you, I know it. Okay, I suppose I have no idea of all the things I really don't know, but, hopefully, I'm getting smarter. It means a lot to me to know that you're standing by me, in the background, ready to help if I need it. Just don't step in too soon, and if you have to step in, don't be too heroic. And please don't rub my nose in my mistakes. That never helps.

I Need Your Affection

Here's another tricky one. Obviously, I don't need you constantly running up to me in front of my friends and giving me great big hugs. On the other hand, I don't need you to keep me at arm's length either. I'm sure it must sometimes feel like a tightrope to walk, Mom. Join the club.

I remember how I used to fight baby sister to sit in the front seat next to you. I remember how I loved to hold your hand when we walked through the mall. No offense, Mom, but those days are gone. Unless I'm desperate to entice you to buy me something, that's probably not going to happen again. Sorry, but it's the truth. It feels good to know that you still love me, but we need to come up with more subtle ways of showing it.

TEN TRAITS I ADMIRE MOST IN YOU

1. Your acceptance of who I am and who I'm becoming.
2. Your ability to not take life too seriously.
3. Your patience, even when I'm being a brat.
4. Your kindness when I don't deserve it.
5. Your words of wisdom when I need them (without overdoing it).
6. Your respect for me as a person and for my choices.
7. Your interest in my activities (without being too obvious).
8. Your stability, dependability, and general grown-upness.
9. Your honesty (but not when you're painfully honest).
10. Your advice (when asked).

Here are a few crib notes. A pat on the back can say a lot, especially if I've had a rough day, but a pat on the head can feel demeaning. It's reassuring when you put your hand on my shoulder, but not for too long and definitely not when my friends are around. Small gestures go a long way these days, Mom, even if it's just a kind word or an encouraging e-mail or even a note slipped under my bedroom door that says, "I love you." Just don't do it when anyone is looking, okay? You get it, don't you, Mom?

I Wish for Your Wisdom

I know, it's not like I go around saying, "Wow, my mom is so wise." (Don't you wish?) I know you are wiser than I am, but I'm not so dumb either. Will I ever admit this aloud? You know the answer. Maybe in ten years.

It feels good to see you do something or say something that's wise. It's kind of reassuring and gives me hope that I might become wiser too. Here's the thing about wisdom, Mom: it's usually quiet and humble. When I see parents trying to appear smart, they usually come off as pompous show-offs—the kind of parents that teens tease (behind their backs, of course). I don't want you to be that parent.

I do like it when you gently point something out to me and it's obvious that you know what you're talking about. Like the other day when Madison and I were in the kitchen getting a soda and you mentioned that you had decided to quit buying bottled water because you'd just heard about how many bazillions of plastic bottles are piling up in landfills. Well, it might seem like no big deal, but after you left, Madison said, "Your mom's right. We should do the same thing." That was cool, Mom, and a good reminder to me that you're smarter than I give you credit for.

I Want Your Patience

The fact is, I really need you to be patient with me. I'm sure you're thinking that I'm your greatest challenge when it comes to having patience. I know I try your patience. I've heard you complain about it. I know you sometimes think that I do it on purpose. Okay, maybe sometimes I do, especially when you're being demanding. I guess I like to give it back in spades.

But here's a heads-up: when you try to be patient with me, I try a little harder to take it easy on you. I remember when I was a kid and you tried to get me to count to ten before I lost my temper. Well, you might try the same thing. Sometimes it helped me. Sometimes it still helps.

I'm trying to grow up, Mom. It just takes time. It also takes a few mistakes, a few stepped-on toes, and maybe even a dented fender or two. If this whole thing were up to me, I'd be grown-up already. It's not like I enjoy the painful struggles of getting there. It's not like I relish humiliation or these feelings of insecurity, self-doubt, and sheer terror.

It will help me if you can take a long, deep breath and trust that things will eventually get better.

FIVE

YOU SAY YOU LISTEN

BUT SOMETIMES I JUST NEED TO BE HEARD

'm sure you know how it feels when I don't listen to you (since you point out that I don't on a regular basis), but do you know that's how I feel too? You say you listen, but I can tell when you're not. Why should I try to talk to you if you're not listening? I'm just wasting my breath. (Hey, I stole that line from you!)

If communication is such a big deal (isn't that what you're always telling me?), why are you so bad at it? Okay, I'll admit that I'm not so great at it either, but I'm a kid. I'm still learning. Besides, my friends don't seem to have a problem understanding me. They know how to listen, for the most part anyway. Sometimes they're just like you—self-absorbed and just pretending. For that matter, so am I.

I realize there are times when you really do want to listen to me, so much so that you pester me to talk to you. You ask all kinds of obnoxious questions and then accuse me of being moody because I don't want to talk at that particular moment. Your timing is off. The more you bug me, the more I will clam up. Take a hint, Mom, and just wait.

If something is gnawing at me, it might take a while before I sift through it and am ready to actually talk about it. Maybe I never will. If you've hurt my feelings, which is often the case, I might need time to heal before we can start hashing it out. There are some things that cannot be forced from a teen. Conversation is one of them.

Reverse Psychology Helps...

Here's a tip, a clever trick you used on me when I was younger and you wanted me to comply with your wishes. *Reverse psychology.* I'll admit that, when done right, it still works. Not only that, but I occasionally even use it on you, and you fall for it.

But I'll warn you, Mom, it only works on me if you're very cautious and not too obvious about the whole thing. Seriously, you need to handle this one with care. If you go all theatrical and psychological on me, it will explode in your face, and you will end up looking lame.

What I'm suggesting is just a quiet nonchalance. You act somewhat interested in engaging with me, but you apply no pressure. Like, hey, I can either talk to you or not. No big deal. In other words, you make me feel as if I am the one who is choosing to engage. When it's my choice, I will feel freer to express myself in a genuine way.

So Does Body Language

Because I'm a teen and somewhat self-absorbed, I'm sure you assume that I pay no attention to nonverbal communication, like body language. Wrong. I may try to hide it, but I'm watching, and a lot of times your body language is communicating all sorts of things to me. Do you wonder what messages you're sending, without even meaning to? A sigh, your arms folded across your chest, a creased forehead, tight lips, your hand raking through your hair, a sideways glance, or your hands on your hips all add up to something. Of course, my math could be wrong, but these are some of the messages I get from you and some of the reasons I don't always attempt to communicate:

- *I'm busy.*
- *I'm tired.*
- *I have to do everything myself.*
- *You are a selfish brat.*
- *No one appreciates me.*
- *I don't have time for this.*
- *I'm angry.*

So maybe you need to take a look at yourself, Mom. You might want to ask yourself whether or not you're communicating what you want to communicate. If you see me doing these same things, you might ask yourself who I learned it from. You might be surprised. Or I might be all wet.

Miscommunication Is a Two-Way Street

If communication is a two-way street, so is miscommunication. For instance, let's say you're busy and I know it, like last Wednesday. Do you remember when I casually asked if Madison could come over? You absentmindedly nodded, hinting that I should get out of your hair, then you turned back to face your computer. Later you realized that Madison was spending the night (on a school night) and came unglued. I patiently pointed out that I had asked and you had given me permission. Then you impatiently pointed out that you meant something else. Two-way street, Mom. We miscommunicated. Unfortunately for you, I came out on top. Really, you should say what you mean and mean what you say. Hmm, where have I heard that before?

Now, you might say the whole dilemma occurred because I,

THINGS I'LL NEVER SAY WHEN I'M A MOM

* "Because I said so."
* "While you live under my roof, you'll live by my rules."
* "I'll treat you like an adult when you start acting like an adult."
* "There's a place for everything."
* "I hope someday you have children just like you."
* "I didn't ask who made the mess. I said to clean it up!"
* "Do you think I'm made of money?"
* "I don't care who started it."
* "Money doesn't grow on trees."
* "You call this music?"

your conniving teenage daughter, was being deceitful and trying to trick you. But, hey, I'm a teenager. Isn't that what I do? Besides, I had a very good reason, a reason you never heard because you were too grumpy to listen. But if you had been able to listen, I would've told you that Madison's mom and stepdad were in the middle of their worst fight ever, and Madison was very upset and needed a safe place to crash. Besides that, we actually did homework that night, and we didn't even stay up late.

* "You don't need a reason why."
* "Just wait until your dad hears about this."
* "How many times do I have to tell you?"
* "Don't get smart with me."
* "You're not going out in that, are you?"
* "Act your age!"
* "Get the hair out of your eyes."
* "Stand up straight."
* "Would you jump off a bridge just because your friends were doing it?"
* "Don't talk back to me."
* "If I've said it once, I've said it a thousand times."

Listen

Okay, you're probably thinking, *There she goes again acting immature, rude, and selfish.* Well, I'm just being honest, Mom. This is how I feel sometimes. Like you'll go on and on about something and totally miss the point. Does that stop you? I don't think so.

Here's a hint: when you're droning on and you observe me with that blank expression—eyes glazed over, arms crossed over my chest, a frown on my face—get a clue. I am not listening. Chances are, you weren't either.

Remember the time you called me on the carpet because you were appalled at the charges on my cell-phone bill? "This is unacceptable," you began in your *I am not losing control* voice. "I knew you were too young and too irresponsible for a cell phone. Kids get in over their heads all the time with these phones. The only reason I got it for you was for emergencies. Well, you can be certain it'll be turned off now. And I expect you to do extra chores around here, unless you'd like to get a part-time job, not that you can afford to slide on your studies, since your grades aren't—" On and on you rambled in this nagging voice, never letting me say a word.

I'm guessing you rehearsed the whole spiel on your way home from work, or maybe you used a cheat sheet with a list of judgments against me that you had hidden in the palm of your hand. Whatever the case, I picked up the phone bill and examined it as you continued to blow off steam. Finally, you paused and I said, "Mom, I can explain—"

"The only thing I want you to explain is how and when you plan to pay for this. Money doesn't grow on trees, you know, and

just because you're a kid doesn't mean you don't have to take responsibility for your own—"

"Shut up!" Okay, that probably wasn't the smartest thing to say.
It just escaped my lips.

"How dare you speak to me like—"

"Be quiet and listen," I pleaded with you. Then, following your
example, I began to speak so quickly that you couldn't get a word in
edgewise. I pointed out that I didn't even know two of the most frequently called phone numbers, the numbers that had sent the phone
bill sky high. As it turned out, baby sister (jealous because she didn't
have a cell phone) had been borrowing mine. She'd been practicing
text messaging her girlfriends.

Anyway, you get my point. Sometimes parents just need to zip
it and listen. Okay, I admit I need to do that too.

Don't Take Me Too Seriously

I know I can be a drama queen sometimes. I can blow things out of
proportion, or as you sometimes say, "Make a mountain out of a
molehill." I think that's an exaggeration on your part.

Here's what I suggest. Why not scale down your reaction and
not take me so seriously? I mean, you know I'm a teenager and I
might go off about something that's not that important, so why not
just accept that, instead of overreacting? In the end, wouldn't we both
be happier? Maybe if you didn't overreact, my little storms would
blow over more quickly and leave much less damage in their wake.

On the other hand, I don't want you to start ignoring me. Sometimes I do have a serious point and need to be heard. I guess you'll

just have to rely on your motherly intuition to discern the difference between a real problem and a production.

Give Me a Break!

Here's a real conversation killer, Mom. It's something we teens make fun of when our parents aren't around. It's those really dumb things that spill out of your mouth when your mind is on a break, or maybe you're taking a mental health day and left your brain at the office. Like when you say, "Do you think I'm made of money?" Yeah, right. I look at your face, and I see Ben Franklin and dollar signs looking back at me. Get real. Or how about, "Were you born in a barn?" I mean, weren't you there when I was born? *Duh.*

I guess they're parental clichés, but do you really think we're listening to them? Do you think they do any good? Did your parents say junk like that to you? If they did, which I guess is the case, did you listen? My bet is you were just as checked out then as we are now, but somehow those little pieces of wit and wisdom slipped into the gray matter to pop out and haunt us all later.

Anyway, Mom, why not avoid passing along this genetic trait? Otherwise, get ready for me to question your reasoning when you tell me to put a sweater on, despite the fact that it's eighty degrees outside. Or when you say something like, "Because I told you so!" Seriously, Mom, can't you hear how lame that sounds?

I'll admit that communication goes straight down the toilet when we both get angry, but sometimes I don't care. It's like I have this need to toss something out there, even if it's a grenade that will blow up in my face.

I have no doubt that I invited some of the nastiest confrontations we've endured, but I'm the teenager here. What did you expect? Sure, I'll say something stupid or mean or both, spouting off in my general ignorance. Usually it's because I'm feeling bad about myself or because I've just experienced some form of devastation. Maybe I even wanted to talk to you about it, but that's impossible once our tempers flare.

Naturally I've taken you by surprise. I realize you might be tired or grumpy, and in the heat of the moment, you let your guard down and snap back at me. Bad move, Mom. As you know, not only will nothing good come out of this, but I will often use your anger to deflect attention away from myself. Consequently, any possibility for meaningful communication has died a horrible death.

Sadly, you may never know what was eating me, and due to the fireworks, I might even blame you for the whole thing. What if I had something really serious to talk to you about? What if I'd been unfairly accused of something at school? What if my best friend was in jail for shoplifting? What if I was feeling worthless and had a bottle of sleeping pills under my pillow? What if I'd been the victim of date rape?

Okay, maybe I sound a little dramatic again, but these things happen. These are the kinds of things that I need to tell my mother. Unfortunately, I don't always have the skills to calmly introduce a tough subject, so the next time you see me flying off the handle, why not step back, take a deep breath, and ask what's going on?

Hopefully it won't be any big deal, but if it is, won't you be glad you remained calm?

SIX

WHY I NEED SECRETS AND PRIVACY

AND TIME TO MYSELF

Keep out means keep out! We have doors in our house for a reason, right? When mine is closed, it's because I want you— and the rest of the planet—to stay out. Perhaps I should do what I did in grade school and post a sign that reads, KEEP OUT! You thought that was amusing then, but it would probably irritate you now. The point is that I need privacy. Why can't I make you understand this? And why do you assume that, if you lightly tap on my door, you have the right to burst in like you own the joint? When I challenge you on this, you get all defensive and say things like, "Well, this is my house. I have the right to go into any rooms if I want to."

What's that supposed to mean? I don't have rights? It's not really my room? *Your* house isn't *my* house too? Do you want me to live on the streets? I don't think so, but sometimes that's exactly what I feel like doing when you invade my privacy. How would you like it if I tapped on your bedroom door just before crashing in on you? Not that I would do that. Eeew!

Leave Me Alone

Sometimes I just need time to myself. I know you don't totally get this, since you sometimes accuse me of being addicted to my friends and my phone and text messaging and e-mail—blah-blah-blah. You might be surprised to discover that I just need to be alone. Sometimes I need to chill and—don't fall over—*think*. I'm sure I think a lot more than you realize. The fact is, there's a lot to figure out in my life, and sometimes that takes effort and privacy.

Believe it or not, at times I need a quiet place to pray. Okay, you probably think I'm just saying this to get you to back off, but it's the truth. Remember that Jesus said to go into your closet to pray? Well, my closet is too messy, so please give me some space.

My day can be filled with noise and chaos and stress, and sometimes I need a break. Sure, maybe my music is on and it's too loud (for your taste), but maybe it helps me clear my head. What's wrong with that?

Here is my compromise on this issue. If I begin spending way too much time by myself, or if I begin cutting myself off from my friends, or if I push you too far away, maybe it's time to become concerned. Before you make an appointment for me with your favorite shrink, though, why not just ask me what's going on? (But not after you've barged into my room without knocking or being invited. That's always a bad way to initiate a real conversation.)

Sometimes I need privacy, even when I'm not in my room. Just because I'm watching TV or being transported to school or eating my breakfast does not mean it's open season for tapping into my brain. Remember when we talked about body language? Well, try to read my face, Mom. If I am deep in thought, head down, and maybe frowning, ask yourself if this is the best time to intrude into my life. Maybe it is. Maybe you have some vital piece of information you need to communicate to me. Sure, go for it. But you can't always expect me to give you the response you're looking for.

"Can you hear me?" you sometimes demand, like you honestly think I've mysteriously gone deaf. Of course, I can hear you. I only wish I couldn't hear you quite so well. "Are you listening to me?" you persist. I give you a faint nod, but that isn't good enough. It's like you think we've both joined the army. You're Sergeant Mom, and I'm the new recruit who needs to stand up, salute, and say, "Sir, yes, sir!" You say, "Jump," and I should say, "How high?"

Look, Mom, I know there are times when you want me to back off from bugging you about something. As frustrating as it is to not get your attention when I want it, I've learned that it's smarter to wait for a more opportune moment. Okay, I might not always practice this, but I'm a teen. You're the mom. You should be better at this kind of thing than I am.

Stay Outta My Stuff

I realize that some parents have the weird notion that it's their responsibility to snoop in their kids' things. You hear the alarming news of school shootings, meth addiction, reckless sexual behaviors among teens, self-mutilation, huffing, or whatever the latest craze is, and suddenly you're freaking out. Do you think you can prevent this kind of madness in your own house by searching your teen's room? Well, think again, Mom.

For starters, if I was going to do something nutty like blow up the school or whatever, I'm sure I would hide the evidence so well that you'd never find it. Besides, your invasion of my privacy—going through my things—will send only one strong message: *you do not trust me.* Do you know how that feels? It's bad enough when you make me feel like this is your house (not mine), and my room isn't really my room (because you have the right to invade at will), but when you rummage through my personal things, I begin to feel more like an inmate than a member of this family. Can you get that?

Madison told me that her mom actually *read* her diary. The funny thing is, Madison suspected this would happen, so you know what she did? She wrote all kinds of crazy things in her diary. She wrote about having sex with several guys a day and how she sometimes even charged them for it. She wrote that she thought she might be pregnant and stuff like that. Well, her mom totally lost it. She screamed, and then she broke down and cried. All the while, Madison acted as if it were all true. Finally, Madison couldn't take it anymore. She burst into laughter and told her mom that the joke was on her and that she deserved it.

What's my point? It's that if you really can't trust me, Mom, if you really think I'm up to something dangerous or crazy, why not just ask me? But don't do it in a suspicious or accusatory way. Wait until it seems like we're on the same page, then ask me nicely. You might even begin like this: "Hey, I was just reading about a sixteen-year-old girl who used a razor blade to cut herself. It was so sad. I don't really know much about that sort of thing, but if anyone you knew was doing that, I hope we could talk about it. I would want to help, if I could."

That's the best way to get into a teen's head, Mom, not by playing Spy Mom or Nazi Mom or Prison Warden Mom. None of those roles inspire your daughter to open up to you. If anything, they push us to want to break the rules, to do something bad just to show you. Remember what Madison did? Well, she's still pushing the envelope in her real life too. Maybe not to the extent she wrote about in her diary, but who knows what she might do if her mom keeps sneaking around and going through her stuff.

WAYS TO TOTALLY ALIENATE ME FROM YOU

* walk into my room without knocking
* eavesdrop on me and my friends
* remove the door to my room (I know a mom who did this!)
* read my e-mail messages
* snoop in my room under the guise of putting laundry away
* listen to my phone messages
* read my journal (this is the worst!)
* go through my backpack just because I left it out
* spy on me while I'm on a date
* snoop through my homework
* talk to my friends' parents about me

Lighten Up

I know parents of teens experience a certain amount of paranoia and question what might go wrong. I guess that's natural. In a way, I go through a similar paranoia—only it's more about me. Here's a bit of good news, Mom: most of the kids I know are *not* messed up, at least not seriously. Sure, we all have our problems, but statistically, more of us are on track than parents realize. Maybe that's because the media blows stories out of proportion, scaring us all to death.

Chances are, I'm not going to do anything so terrible that it will ruin my life. Oh, I'm sure that some of my choices are impacting my life, maybe even more than I realize. Was it any different for you? Could your parents prevent you from doing crazy things? My guess is they couldn't, and it'll be the same for you.

So why not lighten up? Why not just chill and hope for the best? Besides lightening up, chilling, and hoping for the best, you can pray. Remember that Jesus said we're not supposed to worry about stuff, but to pray. So, instead of getting yourself worked up and freaked over what you're afraid I might be doing (when I'm probably not doing anything), why don't you just shoot up some prayers for me? I'm pretty sure that'll be a whole lot more helpful in the long run.

Go Away

If I've said it once, I've said it a thousand times (sound familiar?): when I'm with my friends, I prefer that you leave us alone, Mom. Just go away and find something else to do, okay? Call up one of your friends, go bowling, or bake a cake. When I'm hanging with friends, whether it's in my room or somewhere else in the house, I really want my space. If we're in your way, you can always nicely suggest we take it elsewhere. Otherwise, can you just make yourself scarce?

My friends and I have important things to talk about. Okay, I hear you snickering. You're thinking, *Yeah right. What do teens discuss that's so important?* It's true, though. To put it into parental language, we are developing social and communication skills, while practicing for that wonderful era you call adulthood. Not that we'd ever describe hanging together like that. *Puleeze.* Do you get the message? We need our space and privacy to figure things out.

We especially need you to become scarce if we're talking about boys. Honestly, Mom, I so do not need to worry that you're lurking around and eavesdropping when I'm telling Madison about my latest crush and how I think he may want to ask me out. I so do not need you asking, "Who is he?" or, "How old is he?" or, "Who are his parents?" or whatever pops into that parental head of yours. If I bring up the subject when we're alone, then I will understand if you have questions. Until then, please just go away.

Mom, do you remember a certain girl you knew in high school? She was that obnoxious girl who always wanted to hang with you and your friends even though you didn't really want her around. She would pester you and lurk around the fringes and offer comments that were, well, weird.

Sometimes that's you, Mom. I hate to say it, but when you try to slip yourself into the conversation with me and my friends, you can look totally lame. It makes me hurt for you. It really does. At the same time, I want to scream.

You need to learn how to bug off. I know those are hard words to hear. Maybe in one of your kinder moments, you can just call it tough love. (You like that phrase.) It's seriously in your best interest to bug off sometimes.

Just Chill

I realize that some of this privacy talk could sound offensive to you. My point is not to hurt your feelings, because I really do love you, and I know you fondly recall those times when I was your little girl and loved having you as part of my world. I mean, you were the center of my world.

I can understand that it's probably hard on you to see that I've changed, that I keep pushing you away. But get real, Mom. What are the options here? Did you think I wasn't going to grow up? Did you really hope that I'd be slow to grow up? I mean, maybe if I were mentally impaired I could remain your little girl forever. But I have a feeling you might not like that either.

So, here's the deal: take a step back, Mom. Take a nice, deep, calming breath and accept that I need this kind of room to grow up. I need space to become my own person. Hopefully, I will become the kind of person you always dreamed I would be.

Here's some really good news: I've heard that once I get past this awkward adolescent stage, we might actually become friends again. I might, once again, confide in you. I might ask you for advice. I might ask you to help me plan my wedding and eventually baby-sit my children. Hey, it could happen.

My guess is it will happen a lot more naturally if you can figure out how to just chill. If you could distance yourself without becoming offended, it would be extremely helpful to both of us. Think about it, okay?

This is a good time for you to invest in your own social life, your own interests, your own relationships. Who knows what you might discover along the way? Here's another news flash, Mom: I don't mean to alarm you, but I've heard that overly protective mothers, the ones who are too wrapped up in their kids' lives, go through this really horrible thing called empty-nest syndrome. I wouldn't want that to happen to you, so take my advice for a change and just chill.

SEVEN

YOUR LECTURES DON'T WORK

AND HERE'S WHY

t's funny how you assume to know more about communication than I do. You think you know more because you're the adult. Still, you occasionally resort to the most archaic form of speech: lecturing. Oh, I'm sure you don't think you're lecturing, but trust me, Mom, you are.

When you go on and on without allowing me to comment, *it is a lecture.* The other sign that you're lecturing is when there's a bubble above my head with a string of *zzzz*'s inside it. I know how to recognize a lecture when I hear one, because that's the way some of my old-fashioned teachers like to teach. Believe me, it's not the most effective way to get your point across. Did I mention that it's also boring?

What happens when you are subjected to a lecture? Like what if your mother or boss or best friend suddenly breaks into a mind-numbing lecture that was directed at you? You don't exactly sit up straight, clasp your hands together, and think, *Oh boy, this is going to be great!*

By the way, statistics fail to impress me. Oh, you might think it's interesting that, say, one out of three teen girls will have sex before she's fifteen, but I'm not impressed. For one thing, where do you get these numbers? For another thing, who cares about stupid stats? I am not a number.

Do you think the kids who are surveyed actually tell the truth? Remember Madison's diary? That was totally bogus, but her mom took it seriously. So really, why pay so much attention to dumb statistics? Why relay such boring information? If you want me to pay attention, think of a new approach, okay?

Talk to the Hand

Here's another way you can get me to tune out, Mom. You hear on the news about the latest teen craze, and you assume I'm going to do it. Like last week when you asked me about mattress surfing. Get real, Mom. Do you honestly think I even know a person who would tie a mattress to the back of a pickup and ride it? It's like you think we're all a bunch of idiots just because we're teenagers. I mean, sure, we do some dumb things—but mattress surfing?

Last week you asked me about branding. I said, "What?" and you explained how one of your friends told you that teens are using a hot piece of metal to brand themselves. Okay, how certifiable is that? I don't like pain, remember? Stop worrying that I'll do something nutty like branding, tattooing, or purposely maiming myself in some horrid way. Unless I give you good reason, I hope you'll think better of me than that. Okay, sometimes I want to get another piercing, but that's normal. It's not like I'm planning to get horns attached to my skull. Seriously, some kids are doing this.

Anyway, the next time you bring up some totally weird and bogus teen trend, think again, or get ready to talk to the hand.

Don't You Dare!

Has it ever occurred to you that when parents make too big a deal over these crazy teen trends, it could backfire? Like when an indignant mother declares, "As long as I'm alive and breathing, no daughter of mine will ever pierce her bellybutton or any other body part!" Well, that's a challenge and a dare. To a teenager, that sounds like an invitation. A teen might interpret that to mean, *Hey, she expects me*

TEN WAYS TO MAKE ME TUNE OUT

1. Launch into your lecture mode.
2. Spout statistics I don't care about.
3. Compare me to teens who act like idiots.
4. Tell me about something that's totally irrelevant to me.
5. Talk to me while I'm watching TV or working on the computer.
6. Give me ultimatums.
7. Act like you know more about teens than I do.
8. Talk to me when I'm on the phone.
9. Talk to me as if I have the mental capacity of a five-year-old.
10. Assume I'll do something just because it's reported in the news.

to do something wild and can't wait to tell her friends that I've gone and done [fill in the blank]. Why go there?

Don't forget. You're talking to a teenager who thinks of rebellion as a way of life. We love doing daring things. Bring it on!

I Can't Hear You

When you go on and on about something, your voice begins to sound like white noise. It puts me to sleep. If you really want me to hear you, don't drone on. Just talk to me.

Do you remember how the grownups were portrayed in the Charlie Brown movies we watched at holiday time? We never saw their faces, and when they spoke, their voices sounded like out-of-tune horns: "Wada-wada-blada-blada-wa-wa-wa." They lectured, and their kids didn't listen. Surely you don't want to be like those cartoon parents, do you, Mom?

If you really want me to listen to you, speak to me in a language I can understand and relate to. Ask me questions that are relevant but not accusatory. Tell me something meaningful that happened to you when you were my age.

There are no guaranties here, but your chances of being heard will improve by at least 70 percent.

See, Mom, I remember how you like statistics.

EIGHT

JUST BECAUSE I SAID, "NOTHING"

DOESN'T MEAN I ACTUALLY MEANT IT

How many times have you asked me, "What's wrong?" and I've just shrugged and said, "Nothing," in a sulky tone? Then you give me that questioning look like you're not convinced and let it go. That could be a mistake. Or not. It just depends.

I know it's my fault you give up so easily. I'm always telling you to give me space, to back off, and to respect my privacy. I've done my best to train you to butt out of my life, but don't forget, Mom, I'm a complex young woman, a dichotomy, a mystery, a conflict about to happen. I might occasionally need you to butt in.

So how do you know when it's time to persist and when it's time to cut me some slack? Well, it's tricky. I'm not even sure I can answer that one. Again, maybe you need to read my body language. I admit that it's probably subtle. If I say, "Nothing's wrong," and I don't look at you or cross my arms like I'm mad or focus on something else, I probably really do mean that nothing's wrong.

But if I give you the slightest sideways glance or make any kind of brief eye contact, I could be giving you a clue that I need to be pressed—gently. (Or I could have something in my eye. Take your chances.) If you persist, ever so gently, and I begin to talk, you should probably pay attention and bite your tongue.

Better yet, don't react at all, because when I'm really troubled about something, even the slightest reaction can shut me down.

Okay, it might not seem that what's bothering me is a big deal, but it might be.

For instance, do you remember the time I told you I was worried about my body and how it didn't seem to be developing like other girls' bodies? Well, that wasn't exactly an easy thing for me to say. Do you remember how you reacted? You quickly assured me that everything would be fine in time. I might've acted like that was a satisfactory answer, but it wasn't. You never gave me a chance to say what was bugging me, so I kept it to myself. Do you have any idea what might be bugging me about myself?

Consider the Possibilities

I think you've forgotten how teen girls obsess over their bodies, their hair, their skin, even their toenails. Maybe it wasn't like that when you were a teen. Maybe you weren't as bombarded as we are with picture-perfect images. I touched on this stuff earlier, but it bears repeating. Keep in mind that there is an enormous list of concerns a girl like me might have. They could include:

- My hair is too thin, too thick, too limp, or too curly.
- I need a perm, a haircut, straightening, or maybe even a wig.
- My hair color is wrong. Can I change it?
- My eyes are too close together, too small, too slanted, or too far apart.
- I want those colored contacts, so that my eyes will be blue instead of hazel.

- My eyebrows are a mess. Should I pluck them, shave them, or wax them?
- Do I need Botox?
- I want lip injections. All my friends are getting them for Christmas.
- What is wrong with my complexion? Can I see a dermatologist or wear a mask?
- I need lots of makeup. Where do I start? How much is too much?
- My ears are too big. Can I fix them?
- My teeth are crooked. I don't want braces. Maybe I need caps.
- My neck is all wrong. Everyone calls me giraffe girl. What can I do?
- I am fat. (Don't tell me I look fine.) What should I do? Go on a diet? Exercise more? Work on an eating disorder?
- My boobs are too small, too big, lopsided, too far apart, or too floppy.
- Where do I go to get cleavage? Can I get a boob job or a Wonderbra?
- My butt is too big, too small, or too flabby.
- What do I do about this strange smell in my armpits, on my feet, and in other private places? No one else smells this bad.
- Why do I have hair on my stomach?
- My arms look like ape arms.

- I have zits on my back. How can I get rid of them?
- My feet are ugly. My toenails look like claws. Can I get a pedicure?
- Should I get a tummy tuck?
- I need liposuction ASAP.

Do you see my problem, Mom? If I tell you about something that's troubling me, I make myself totally vulnerable. I'm already insecure enough. Even though I might hide it or laugh it off, I hate feeling vulnerable. If you handle my confession wrong, it's all over. If I mention one of these problem areas—something that might seem small to you but really matters to me—and you chuckle and say, "Oh, don't worry, honey, you'll outgrow that…yada-yada…," well, I want to magically erase what I just told you and disappear. Instead, I just tune you out.

Please don't make me sorry that I opened my mouth, because if you do, you can be sure I won't be telling you any more embarrassing secrets. That door will close.

Don't Talk About Me

When you trivialize me or act as if I'm blowing something out of proportion, you make me feel like I'm about five years old. That does not feel good. Here's the deal: if you make the effort to listen to the stuff that's troubling me—if I reveal these things to you—why would you want to wreck it all by acting like it's no big deal? Then if I get mad at you for being insensitive, you make fun of me for overreacting. It really hurts and erodes my trust in you.

If I've confided something you think is silly, don't divulge my insecurities to anyone else! (I'm not just talking about my friends here, Mom, although that's the *very worst*. I just want to die.) Seriously, you might think you're doing me a favor by asking Aunt Sally, "Don't you think her skin looks okay since her acne has cleared a little? You don't think she needs a dermatologist, do you?" Now, I feel totally betrayed and humiliated.

Look, if you discuss my problems with your friends, our relatives, or Dad, well, you might as well just spit on me, okay? It's one of the worst things you can do to me. It destroys my trust.

This Is a Test

It's a risk when I tell you something that's sensitive to me, so please don't use my confessions against me. I might have a really serious problem to tell you, so I test you with a minor problem to see if you're ready for the big leagues.

If you fail at the little leagues, how will you ever make it to the next level? And trust me, there are some pretty nasty problems going around for girls my age. If you could hear the things I hear in the girls' bathroom, you would probably be shocked. I could be one of these girls with a big problem. If I am, who do you want me to go to for help?

Just so you'll know, I'm listing some of the problems I see around me. I might be dealing with these problems personally, or I might have a good friend who is. Would you be ready to listen and help me, or would you say something totally unfeeling and uncool?

Would you do something to make me shut you out? How would you respond if I told you about the girl who:

- is the victim of bullying and afraid to speak up.
- is a bully.
- cuts herself to relieve emotional pain.
- is bullied in cyberspace.
- gossips and attacks others in cyberspace.
- has a secret Internet romance with a man she's never met.
- puts risqué photos of herself on the Internet.
- is having sex.
- is afraid she's a lesbian.
- is planning to run away.
- has an eating disorder.
- has been sexually abused.
- has no friends.
- has been a victim of date rape.
- is drinking or experimenting with drugs.
- is considering suicide.
- is having sex with a teacher.

I haven't listed everything, Mom, but I wanted you to know what goes on out there in my world. I don't want you to obsess or freak or lecture me. That's not my point. I just want you to be aware of the problems I see every day.

I'm not telling you this stuff so you can go down this list and ask me if I'm "the girl." You should know better, right? I want you to be ready in case I need to talk to you about something serious. It

LINES THAT SHUT ME DOWN

* "Don't worry, sweetie, you're just going through a phase."
* "It's no big deal. Forget about it."
* "Don't be such a drama queen."
* "You're kidding! You're too smart to do something like that."
* "Why do you worry so much about everything?"
* "Everyone feels like that sometimes."
* "Surely, you're just imagining things."
* "Nice girls don't do that."
* "You're not serious!"

LINES THAT HELP ME OPEN UP

* "How did that make you feel?"
* "It seems like you don't want to talk right now, but when you're ready I want to listen."
* "I understand that you're feeling stressed, but I'm not sure why."
* "I remember that it's not always easy being a teenager."
* "How can we work this out together? Do you have a suggestion?"
* "I feel confused by what you're telling me. Have I misunderstood something?"

would be nice if you could avoid overreacting by doing or saying the wrong thing.

If I begin a conversation with, "This girl I know has a problem," bear in mind that this could be a totally fictional person or a real girl. Or this girl could actually be *me*. Whatever the case, do you want to risk shutting me down before I've even begun? So watch what you say and how you react. It might make or break what happens next. If all else fails, you might count to ten (or maybe even a hundred) before you say anything.

On a Serious Note

I don't live under a rock, so I realize some teens do pretty scary things and that it's probably frightening to be a parent of a teen these days. You may even think that gives you the right to intrude into my life, so you can stop me from doing something stupid. That plan will backfire, Mom. If you sneak around, trying to discover what's going on with me, I will probably try to hide things from you.

Honest conversation is probably your best bet, especially if it's timed well. As I've already mentioned, listen to the clues I'm giving you. If I mention something of a fairly serious nature, it probably means I've been thinking a lot about it. Maybe I'm not thinking about engaging in something dangerous myself. Then again, maybe I am.

I've heard that if someone (particularly a teen) mentions suicide, you should take it seriously. You shouldn't call the crazy unit and book me a room (at least I don't think so), but you should calm yourself and attempt a conversation with me. Some teens will say shocking things, stuff like, "I might as well kill myself." A parent might assume that the teen is just being dramatic or trying to get attention, but that may not be the case.

Madison told me about a girl she knew from another school. The girl had been telling her friends that she was going to kill herself (apparently her boyfriend had dumped her, and she couldn't get over it). Madison said no one took the girl seriously because she'd always been a drama queen. The girl actually chugged a bottle of aspirin, and even then her parents didn't take her seriously. Who knew aspirin could kill you? Madison said she didn't think the girl actually wanted to die, but by the time they got her to the hospital, it was too late. The aspirin had already messed up her kidneys and liver. She died the next day.

Okay, I realize that's a pretty sad story. It's risky telling a parent something like that, but maybe parents need to know about this stuff. Madison wondered if the girl might still be alive had her mom taken her to the hospital sooner. I don't know about that. I guess parents have it tough, trying to figure out what's a real risk and what's not.

Maybe it's like the boy who cried wolf just to see if anyone would come to his aid. The hard part is that teens cry wolf too. I guess parents have to get very good at discerning the difference. It probably wouldn't hurt to pray about this stuff too. Maybe God could give you a heads-up when you need it.

NINE

I'M WATCHING YOU

EVEN WHEN YOU'RE NOT LOOKING

've heard you say that I'm overly influenced by my friends' opinions, but do you ever wonder about your influence on me? You probably assume I'm ignoring you most of the time, and I'll concede that's often the case. Sometimes I'm simply trying to *act* like I'm ignoring you, for a variety of reasons. At times, I just need to aggravate you. At other times, I'm hoping to fly below your radar.

Then there are times—when you're not aware—I am watching you. You'd be surprised at the things I observe, Mom—some good things and some, well, not so good.

As much as I hate to admit it, I am influenced by you in both positive and negative ways. As Dr. Phil said, the same-sex parent has the greatest influence over the child. If you see things you don't like in me, maybe you should look at yourself. Okay, that's my interpretation.

I realize it's your responsibility to impart good training and wisdom to me, Mom, but do you think I take you seriously if you don't live by the same standard you set for me? It's like giving me license to ignore you when you tell me one thing and do something different. Like when you tell me to obey traffic laws, then you speed on the freeway. Why shouldn't I do the same?

You've lectured me about not talking on my cell phone while

driving, but I know for a fact that you talk on your phone when you drive. You may say you're a more experienced driver than I am, but I'm not totally convinced.

How about telling me to pick up my things when you leave your stuff all over the place? Okay, maybe you eventually pick up after yourself, but what kind of message is that sending to me? So remember, I am watching you. Before you yell at me about something, make sure you're not setting a bad example. Maybe the worst is when you tell me to be a good friend and how important it is to remain loyal and then I hear you gossiping about your "dear friend" to someone else. How loyal is that?

Hypocrites

One thing that most teenagers can't tolerate is hypocrisy. Okay, I'm not suggesting that teens are immune to hypocrisy, because that's just plain dumb. I'm also not saying that you're a hypocrite, Mom. But just so you know, most teens think their parents are slightly hypocritical—at least sometimes. Maybe it's part of being a grownup. And maybe you can't really help it. I mean I have no idea what it would be like to raise a teenager. Like you have these great expectations that your kid will turn out perfect, and yet you know that you, yourself, are not. It must be tough.

Here's the deal: don't try to act like you're perfect, and don't try to cover up your mistakes. Doing those things will probably make you look even more like a hypocrite. Your best bet is to admit you're not perfect and let it go. Besides coming across as more genuine, you might actually give me hope. Maybe I won't be thinking I have to measure up to some false ideal of perfection.

You know what really catches my attention, Mom? It's when you live up to your own convictions—even when I can tell it's not easy or that it's costing you something. Sure, I may not say anything, but if I see you going out of your way to be the person you believe God is calling you to be, I sit up and take notice. I'm impressed. And I hope that someday I might be more like you. No, I probably won't say that out loud…not yet, anyway. But I will tuck it away in my memory file. And who knows, I might even attempt to imitate you. Hey, it could happen.

Your Relationships

I like to observe you when you're engaged with your friends—if you don't know I'm looking, that is. I like to see how you interact with them. Sometimes you'll let your hair down and act goofy. It's fun seeing that side of you—as long as you don't get too crazy. No teen likes to see her mom acting out of control. That's unnerving, to say the least.

At times, I can tell when your feelings are hurt or you're feeling insecure. I actually feel empathy for you because you remind me of me, and I'm reminded that it might not be that easy being a grownup. It makes me want to hear what's going on with you and your friends, but not as your confidante. I don't think I could handle that. I have enough friends to keep me busy for now.

It's encouraging when I see that you have good friends and

strong relationships. Whether you know it or not, I sometimes make mental notes on ways you interact with your closest friends. I may never admit it, but I probably do try to imitate you. I just do it in my own way.

Little White Lies

Here's another heads-up: if you want me to be honest—and I know you do—you should watch those little white lies you tell. I know that sometimes you think it's the only safe route. Like when your friend shows you her new puffy jacket that makes her look like the Michelin Tire dude and asks if it makes her look fat. You don't want to hurt her feelings. I suppose that kind of white lie might seem excusable.

But what about when Grandma wants you to go with her to visit your great-uncle in the nursing home and you tell her you have plans when you don't? And what about telling Dad you didn't buy anything at the mall and not mentioning the bag I saw in your trunk? Or what about telling me you didn't phone Madison's house to check up on me, when I know for a fact that you did? I called you on it, and you said it was just a little white lie. You said that to keep me from getting upset, but it was too late. I was already upset.

For starters, those little white lies make me lose respect for you. Maybe the worst part is that they make me think that it's okay to tell my own little white lies. I don't always know how to differentiate between a little white lie, a midsize gray lie, and a big, fat black lie. If the distinction is to keep someone from getting upset, then I could tell some whoppers just to keep you calm—and in the dark. Is that what you want?

And just so you know, I do realize that you're only human and that because you do care about others, you sometimes simply want to spare their feelings by *not* stating the whole truth and nothing but the truth. Your motives are good, Mom. But when it comes to me, honesty (wrapped in kindness) is your best policy. And if I see you living like that, I might even try to do the same…in time.

Putting Yourself Last

Okay, here's something you may not think I notice. But I do. What's up with putting yourself last? I mean, how can it be good when you burn yourself out taking care of everyone and then don't have enough energy to take care of yourself? Is that what you want me to do?

I'm not saying I want a mom who's all self-centered (like I can be sometimes), but I don't want a Martyr Mom either. For one thing, it makes you grouchy, and we all suffer. Besides that, it's not healthy. I might only be a teenager, but I know that much. And it might surprise you that I also know that if you use up all your energy without refueling yourself on Jesus, you'll be running on empty.

I heard someone say (maybe it was Oprah) that moms need to be like a passenger on an airplane during an emergency. When the oxygen masks drop down, you put yours on first so you're able to help others. If you don't, you might die, and the person you're trying to help might die too. You have to take care of your own needs first so that you can help others. Don't always put yourself last, Mom. It may seem heroic, but it really doesn't work.

Gossip

I know you don't think I'm paying attention when you're talking to Grandma or your friends or your sister, but it's like my ears really tune in as soon as you guys start to gossip. Why is that? Maybe it's because you tell me it's wrong to gossip. I heard you tell Grandma about the neighbor who is cheating on her husband and probably getting a divorce. Why don't you consider that gossip? Why don't you call it gossip when you tell Aunt Sue that you saw so-and-so doing such-and-such? When I asked you if something I heard you say was gossip, you said you were simply relaying information, that it was something everyone already knew.

How am I to know the difference between gossiping and relaying information? How can I respect you for getting on my case for gossiping when you do the same thing? Maybe we both need to watch it.

Stressed Out

I'm also watching you when you get stressed out. I can't always see it coming, but suddenly it's like you're a kettle that's been left on the burner too long and ready to boil over. Naturally, I try to make myself scarce about then.

Why do you let yourself get that stressed out? Aren't there ways to prevent that from happening? I realize we can't always control the stress that comes into our lives, but there must be ways to reduce some of it. From my vantage point, it sometimes appears that you invite stress—like you thrive on it. That worries me.

Do you know that stress can make you sick? It can make people around you pretty miserable too. So why not take measures to prevent it? When someone asks you to do something you clearly don't

THINGS I'VE CAUGHT YOU DOING THAT MADE ME PROUD

* being generous to a stranger
* holding your tongue when I know you want to blast someone
* being kind to one of my friends
* telling the truth, even when it's not easy
* saying no to an activity that would stress you out
* changing the subject when your friend starts to gossip
* taking time to listen to a friend who's hurting
* not criticizing yourself when dinner's less than perfect
* reading your Bible
* taking time to care for yourself
* letting someone go ahead of you in traffic
* helping a neighbor who's experienced a loss

*

have time to do, why not just say no? Are you afraid someone won't like you if you decline?

Here's the deal, Mom, when you agree to do too much and take on things you don't have time for, it's like a slap in the face to your family. You're choosing to give your best self, your best patience, and your best humor to people who don't even live under your roof.

Putting Yourself Down

You probably don't realize I'm paying attention when you put your-self down. You may even think it's okay, because I put you down too, especially when I'm mad or frustrated or just trying to be funny. I admit I do that. In my defense, I plead adolescence. However, it's one thing for me to put you down and totally different for you to put yourself down.

It hurts me when you put yourself down. For instance, the other day I overheard you say, "I'm so stupid!" Later that day, I saw you looking at yourself in the mirror. You frowned and said, "My thighs are so fat!" I felt bad. Then I went to my mirror to look at my own thighs. After all, we share the same DNA. Maybe my thighs are fat too, and I just never noticed. Now I have one more thing to add to my hate list.

Can you see where this is going, Mom? Can you see how, if you're my example, it's not encouraging for me to hear you say that you're not good enough? I mean, you keep assuring me that I'll feel better about myself when I'm grown-up, but you seem to be stuck in the very same rut. Trust me, that is not very reassuring, and I don't think it's good for you. When people (including your family) hear you making these statements, they might begin to believe it. If you confess, "I'm such a rotten cook," we all start complaining about dinner. For my sake, why not cut the put-downs? If you really need to pick on yourself, just spend some time with a sarcastic teenager.

Values

You may not realize that one of your greatest areas of influence in my life is your values. When you don't compromise your convictions, when you live by your beliefs, I can't help being impressed. Oh, I probably won't mention it, at least not in this decade, but it captures my attention and gives me a sense of stability.

Believe it or not, there are parents without values. Okay, maybe they just have really weird values, like putting themselves first or using illegal drugs or cheating on taxes or breaking laws or lying, cheating, stealing, or whatever. These parents are setting the very worst examples for their kids, and I can assure you, Mom, their kids are not happy about it. Sure, their kids are good at covering it up (What teen wants her friends to know that her parents are seriously messed up?), but you can tell that their lives are pretty miserable. I happen to know that some of these kids are attempting to parent their own parents, taking on responsibilities that teenagers shouldn't be responsible for. If that's not upside down, I don't know what is.

I suspect these kids feel adrift on the ocean in a ship with no captain at the helm, rocking and rolling on stormy waves because there's no one steering. It's probably a little scary. I'm thankful that's not me. I appreciate what you're trying to do, Mom. It's impacting me more than either one of us realizes. Thanks.

TEN

I'M NOT AS CONFIDENT

AS MAYBE I APPEAR TO BE

As I said before, I'm getting good at concealing my imperfections. Confidence is the mask I wear. All teens wear it part of the time—to be honest, we probably wear it most of the time. If we took off our masks, you would that see we are shaking in our boots. I know: I just mixed my metaphors. I'm a teen. I'm allowed.

Here's the weird thing about being a teen and lacking confidence: sometimes it seems like moms were put on this planet to search and destroy and totally annihilate all shreds of their teens' confidence. What confidence your mom doesn't destroy, your friends and enemies finish off. At least, that's how it feels.

I step out of my room (after trying on about a hundred different outfits because I really want to look cool), and you say, "You're not wearing that, are you?" I so want to scream. Okay, maybe I do scream. Do you have any idea how those six little words make me feel? I wonder why I bother. Why don't I just give up trying? Why don't I just put on a potato sack and rubber flip-flops and call it a day? Really, Mom, how would you feel if I said that to you? Oh, you'd probably shrug it off, because you've had a lot more time to learn to deal with criticism, but I suspect it would hurt a little.

That might be one of the reasons I pick on you sometimes. I just want to get even. Or maybe I'm just being ornery. Who knows?

They say what goes around comes around. If you dis me on my appearance, I will dis you back. In fact, I'll probably do an even better job of it than you did, because teenagers can be heartless and mean.

You need to be reminded that attacking someone is a defense tactic in the teen world. "Get them before they get us" is a teen survival skill. I can tell that Madison is feeling insecure about her outfit when she points out that Cammie's jeans make her butt look big. It distracts from the fact that Madison thinks her skirt makes her thighs look fat. It's her way of saying, "I'm on top." She won't be on top for long, though, if Cammie notices Madison's skirt. If Cammie is caught off guard and feels bad enough, she might not notice Madison's skirt. She might just slink away and consider skipping lunch.

I'd like to say I don't resort to such mean tactics, but that would be untrue. We all do it, in our own way. Some of us turn fashion critiquing into an art form, while others keep it tucked in their back pockets to pull out when needed.

The Smack Down

It's amazing how little it takes to smack down a teen girl. Just a few words will do the trick. Sometimes all it takes is a critical look. We learn to expect this from other teens—whether it's from our friends or our enemies—but I have to admit that it still surprises me to get smacked down by my own mom. I thought moms were supposed to want their daughters to grow into confident young women. Of course, that's what you want, but have you ever considered how you sometimes do exactly the opposite? Have you ever thought about how many times you've smacked me down in public? You think you're just being a typical mom, and you defend yourself by saying that parenting a teenage girl is the hardest job on earth. My life is so much easier? Being a teen isn't exactly a walk in the park.

What about the time we were shopping for jeans and I really wanted a pair that you insisted was too expensive? I was trying to be nice about it, while pleading my case to help you understand how important these particular jeans were to me. You didn't give my feelings even an ounce of consideration, and you had the nerve to make a huge scene in the department store.

"That's ridiculous," you told me, while I held up the jeans with my most beguiling, hopeful, and imploring expression, which left me vulnerable.

"But I love them," I protested. "They are perfect, totally perfect."

"Look at these jeans. These are nice," you said, pulling a totally lame pair off the rack. I mean, they were so bad my friends would assume I'd bought them at a dollar store.

"They're all wrong, Mom." I clung more tightly to the wonderful jeans, imagining myself wearing them to school the next day, hearing the compliments from my friends, feeling like I was actually worth something. Okay, I know it's superficial to think that your clothes add to your self-worth, but, hey, I'm a teen. What can I say?

"These jeans don't look any different from the expensive ones," you persisted. "In fact, they seem better made than that pair. And they are half the price."

I patiently tried to point out the differences, which I felt were totally obvious. Any of my friends would get it, but you had already decided about the whole thing. If I'd been thinking more clearly, I would've cut my losses and given up right then, but I really wanted those jeans!

"I'll do extra chores at home," I said quietly, noticing that we were now being watched by other shoppers.

You just laughed at me. "Oh honey, you don't even do the chores you're supposed to do now."

"I'll baby-sit to earn the money," I promised.

You laughed again, even louder this time. By this time, several shoppers were watching us. Oh, they were pretending not to, but I could tell.

"Why don't you just try these?" You used your sweet voice as you urged me. Like that was going to work! You thrust the disgusting pair of jeans toward me, expecting me to take them.

"I don't want them," I said, pushing the jeans back at you.

"But you said you needed jeans," you protested in your sweet voice.

"Forget it," I said and walked away.

You continued to make a scene by trying to get me to come back and try on that stupid pair of ugly cheap jeans. Like that was going to happen. Not!

"If you like those stupid jeans so much, Mom," I snapped, "get a pair for yourself. They might be ugly, but they'd probably be an improvement over those granny pants you're wearing now." Naturally, that made you mad.

"You are so spoiled," you said loud enough for the whole store to hear. That was the last straw, and I was so out of there. I guess you thought you'd won that round. You'd smacked me down good—and in public.

What did you win, Mom? You got an angry daughter, stripped of dignity and confidence, who wanted to commit a violent act. Your prize was a hurt daughter who was not speaking and who had lost respect for her mother. Really, was it worth it?

Maybe I was acting spoiled about the jeans. Maybe they were too expensive, but couldn't you have handled it differently? Couldn't you have at least listened to me? There must be something we can do to prevent this from happening again (if I ever agree to go shopping with you again).

Negativity

I know you can't help being negative sometimes. You're only human, and you get tired and fed up and aggravated. You can't always control what comes out of your mouth, but do you know how devastating it is for me to hear you say things like, "You'll never grow up," or, "You are such a slob," or, "You'll never do this right."

These words might seem like innocent comments to you, Mom, but they seriously hurt. Like weeds, they are easily sown but later sprout up as ugly insecurities, low self-esteem, and apathy. Oh sure, I might act like it's no big deal when you say something negative. I might pretend to be shrugging it off, but that's probably not the case.

I'm sure you've heard of a self-fulfilling prophecy. A parent tells a kid she's a mess, and before long she believes it and really is a mess. A parent tells a kid that she'll never amount to anything, and—voilá—she grows up and never amounts to anything.

Does that mean kids can blame all their failures on their parents? Well, yeah, *duh*. I mean, it might not really be the parents' fault, because maybe the kids made some bad choices, but who do you think a teen is going to blame? Herself or her parents? You get one guess.

So ask yourself what your desired outcome is. Do you want to raise a daughter who grows up insecure, incapable, and lacking in confidence? Do you want me to be so unsure of myself that I never leave home? I don't think so. It could happen, though, if you plant too many negative seeds in me. Those weeds could take over.

Don't Kick Me When I'm Down

I'll admit that I sometimes make mistakes. Okay, maybe I make lots of mistakes. There are all kinds of reasons why I make mistakes. Sometimes it's simply a matter of ignorance (mine, that is), and sometimes I just make stupid choices because I'm being stubborn or rebellious.

Usually, my mistakes come with natural consequences. I think that might be God's way of driving a point home so I can learn from my mistakes and not make the same ones again and again. One of the natural consequences—one I really hate—is the embarrassment of blowing it. Whether I blow it at school with my friends or at home, it's kind of humiliating to fail.

It's even worse when someone you thought was in your court, rubs your face in it by saying things like, "I told you so," or, "I thought you knew better than that," or, "I can't believe you were that dumb." Stuff like that.

It's not like I expect you to congratulate me, but a little empathy might be nice. And don't assume that, just because you give me a little empathy, I'll think you are excusing me from whatever I did. I'm not stupid.

Smoke Screens

Do you know what a little empathy might do? For one thing, I wouldn't react to your hostility and get mad at you and, as a result, forget about the consequence I've been dealt.

If you want me to learn from my mistakes (you do, don't you?), the worst thing you can do is give me an excuse to create a smoke screen. That's an easy defense that allows me to shift the focus from me to you, and that's an ideal way for me to avoid the consequences.

If you chastise me unduly—after I've blown it and know it and am already sorry—I will turn the tables on you, and you will suddenly become the target. I'll say things like, "My parents don't understand me," or, "My mom is so mean," or, "Just when I need you, you slap me in the face," or, "If I had different parents, I might not mess up so much." Those are all great smoke screens for disguising whatever it was that got me into this fix in the first place.

So if you want me to learn from my mistakes and deal with them, why not show some empathy and let me know that you can relate? Then maybe we can calmly discuss where I went wrong and how I can avoid doing it again.

Good Enablement

We usually define *enablement* as something bad, but I think there might be a good form of enablement too. Maybe I'm making up a new definition for the term, but I think there are things you can do to enable me to be more confident.

One way I gain confidence is knowing you believe in me. Let's say I decide to apply for my first part-time job, and maybe you think this particular job is more than I can handle. You have a choice. You can say, "I think that job is going to be too hard for you. You don't have the right experience." Or you can say, "You won't know until you try. You're a smart girl. Why not go for it?" How will choosing option one help me? For starters, your choice of words will probably make me more determined to go after that job, but I'll be doubting myself. If I actually get the job, my self-doubts might affect my performance at work.

On the other hand, how would choosing option two hurt anything? Sure, you have your doubts, but you're keeping them to yourself. I go in for the job thinking, *Mom believes in me. She thinks I'm smart. I am smart. I can handle this.* The interviewer senses my confidence, so I get the job. Maybe the job is a challenge, but I feel good about myself. I feel confident, and I figure things out. Worst-case scenario: I don't figure it out and I get fired. At least I won't blame you. And if you're smart, you'll be sympathetic and there will be no "I told you so" to deal with.

WAYS YOU HELP ME BECOME MORE CONFIDENT

* Point out my strengths instead of my weaknesses.
* Allow me to take risks.
* Celebrate my victories without being too obvious.
* Avoid focusing on my failures—and don't throw any pity parties for me.
* Encourage me to try new things.
* Recognize my inner qualities.
* Support my beliefs and convictions.
* Quietly come alongside when I'm facing a particularly hard challenge.
* Don't question my choices in extracurricular activities.
* Don't prod me to do things I'm not ready to do.
* Don't pressure me to apply to your alma mater when I don't want to go there.
* Keep your doubts about me to yourself.

THE PAYOFF

* I learn how to accept my failures as a normal part of life— and hopefully learn from them.
* I grow more confident and consequently make wiser choices.
* I try new things—not dangerous things, but activities that might stretch me and help me to grow.
* I learn to listen to my instincts and possibly avoid some pitfalls.
* I become stronger in my own convictions.
* My faith becomes my own—not my parents' hand-me-down.

ELEVEN

I ALREADY HAVE FRIENDS

I NEED A MOTHER

Yeah, I know I've already mentioned this, but just in case you weren't listening or forgot, I do not need my mother to act like she's my friend. Okay, I don't want you to act like you're my enemy either. I just want you to be my mom.

To be fair, maybe this whole idea of being the mom to an ornery teenage girl leaves you cold or you think it's hopeless or you're worried that you might fail or maybe you feel you've already failed. Well, join the club, Mom. I'm pretty sure there are millions of moms out there who feel just like you.

To be honest, I can't imagine how I'd feel if I were in your shoes, how hard it would be to parent someone like me. Admittedly, it's a thankless job, and I don't think you get combat pay. I guess the good news is that it won't last forever. I might grow up someday.

In the meantime, you need to realize that, although I'm telling you I need a mom and I need you to act like a mom, I probably won't show a whole lot of appreciation when you do.

On the other hand, that doesn't mean I won't notice. Trust me, I see some of those sweet little "mom" things you do for me. I know I'm not a six-year-old, but I still love it when you leave me a quick you-can-do-it note or maybe even a special treat (just not out where my friends can see it). And I appreciate it when I walk into the kitchen to be greeted by warmth and good smells—as well as a cheerful greeting. And sometimes I even like to go shopping with you—especially when you listen to my opinions on style. Okay, you don't need to take fashion advice from me, but I like it when you show me some respect, and that's when I'm more likely to listen to you when you gently suggest that those black leather pants might not be the most practical addition to my wardrobe.

The Jealous Mom

One of my friends, Fergie, has an interesting mother dilemma. Since she's an only child and her parents are divorced, Fergie's mother assumes that Fergie should be her best friend and do everything with her. As I mentioned before, this worked when we were little girls. We loved hanging out with our moms and drank up all the attention they poured on us, but all that changed when we entered adolescence. Unfortunately for Fergie, her mom did not get that memo, so poor Fergie plays a game. She tries to placate her mother by hanging with her and going shopping or to the movies or to lunch. She still wants time to be with her friends, so sometimes, to kill two birds with one stone, she includes her mom with her friends. Big mistake.

For one thing, her friends don't like it. I mean, what teen girl wants someone's mom hanging around while they talk about boys and dating or who did what with whom? To make matters worse, Fergie's mom tries to act cool in order to fit in, as if she thinks we're all glad she's there. Not! Poor Fergie. I can tell she's dying inside.

Fergie doesn't act like herself when her mom's around. She used to be funny and fun to be with, but when her mom's with us, Fergie becomes a ghost girl—she's there, but she's not really there. I feel sorry for her. When her mom's not there, it's not much better because her mom calls her a bazillion times every hour. Fergie is not allowed to turn her phone off. When her mom calls, we can tell she's making Fergie feel guilty for having fun without her. A lot of times, Fergie will just give up and go home so she can be with her pathetic mom.

This saga gets even worse, because her mom says mean things

TEN WAYS YOU COULD RUIN MY LIFE

1. Act like you're just one of the girls when I have friends over.
2. Flirt with my boyfriend.
3. Tell my girlfriends details about your honeymoon.
4. Make fun of me or belittle me in front of my friends.
5. Show my friends my baby photos.
6. Ask my friend if you can try on her new jacket.
7. Try to sound cool by using the latest teen jargon.
8. Send weird text messages to me at school.
9. Tell my friends an off-color or dumb joke.
10. Ask my friend if your jeans make your butt look big.

THE OLD STODGY MOM RULES

* Moms must believe that their teen daughters reflect on them personally—if we look bad, you look bad.
* Moms must monitor whatever comes out of their daughters' mouths—keep that bar of soap handy, Mom.
* Moms must control their daughters' choices in friends.
* Moms must assume full responsibility for their daughters' wardrobes.
* Moms must disapprove of their daughters' first boyfriends, especially when any sign of physical affection is exhibited.
* Moms must take personally everything their teen daughters say in anger.
* Moms must take full responsibility for their daughters' moral character.
* Moms must not have a social life or pursue any activities that might distract them from their parenting responsibilities.
* Moms must show up at every school function and be ready to engage with every person who is involved in their daughters' education.
* Moms must express their opinions on every topic their daughters bring up—get ready to lecture that girl!
* Moms must never trust their daughters. Period.
* Moms must wear frumpy old clothes and orthopedic shoes—think comfort, not fashion.
* Moms must expect the worst when raising teen daughters. You will probably get what you expect.

THE NEW AND IMPROVED MOM RULES

* Moms will accept that teens need to experiment with hair, make-up, and fashion, without taking it too seriously or personally.
* Moms will understand that teens are apt to say inappropriate things sometimes, but it's not the end of the world.
* Moms will not judge their daughters' friends too harshly but instead find out what makes them tick.
* Moms will allow teen daughters freedom to pick out their own clothes—with gentle guidelines.
* Moms won't be too critical of boyfriends but will get to know them.
* Moms will understand that teen tempers express opinions that teens might later regret. Give them time to apologize.
* Moms will acknowledge that they've given their daughters good moral guidance, and their teens will eventually follow it.
* Moms are entitled to a social life, without putting teens at risk.
* Moms will be involved, without making a nuisance of themselves, at their teens' schools.
* Moms will avoid lecturing and will keep certain judgments and opinions to themselves.
* Moms will at least pretend to trust their teen daughters, while keeping their eyes wide open.
* Moms will understand that they can still be somewhat fashionable—just not extreme.
* Moms will expect the best from their teen daughters, and in time, they will probably be rewarded with the best.

about Fergie's friends. She puts them down and makes fun of them. I've actually heard her do this. Fergie says it's just because her mom's jealous and wants Fergie all to herself. I think her mom needs to grow up and get a life with her own friends before she ruins her daughter's life.

It wouldn't surprise me if Fergie ditches her mom someday. She'll probably head off to college and just keep going. Who could blame her?

I'm so glad you're not like that, Mom. When it comes to friends, I need you to have your own friends, and I'll have mine. If we ever share the same friends, we should both be old ladies.

Keep a Healthy Distance Without Checking Out

It probably sounds like I'm asking you to walk a fine line or pull off a balancing act. I never said it was going to be easy, but I think there are things you can do to make it easier.

For instance, you can keep a healthy distance when my friends are around. It's not that I think you'll ever be like Fergie's mom, but I confess to a little paranoia when it comes to my friends. I'm sorry, but that's just normal.

I know I've touched on this already, and I don't want to beat you up about it, but it's important, Mom. If I feel like you're crossing the line with my friends—if you're being intrusive or pushy or embarrassing or you're eavesdropping—I will probably react in one of several possible ways. You might want to ask yourself if this is the outcome you're hoping for before you step over that line.

For starters, I'll probably stop inviting my friends over to our house. That's the easiest way to remedy the problem. I won't want to stop hanging with them, so I'll spend more time at their houses. You will know even less about what I'm doing or who I'm doing it with. I'll also stop asking you for rides. That means you won't always know who is driving. I might tell you one thing but do something else. It happens.

I also might lie to you about my friends. If your interest in my friends is overwhelming or you want me to quit hanging with certain ones, I might lie to get you off my case. Short of hiring a detective, you won't know if I'm telling you the truth or not.

Why not save us both the trouble and give me space when my friends are around? That way you can keep up with what's going on in my life without hiring that detective.

TWELVE

WE MAY HAVE SIMILARITIES

BUT I AM NOT YOU

I'm sure we are more alike than I care to admit, and perhaps someday I'll acknowledge our similarities. In the meantime, you need to remember that I am not you. I'm not even a mini you, nor do I want to be you.

Don't take it personally, Mom, but I *want* to be myself, even if I look like a total mess. Even though you seem to have it all together, I do not want to be you. Can you understand that?

Serena's mom is a real control freak. It's like she is trying to live her life through Serena. Maybe her own teen years weren't so great, and she thinks this is her second chance. She picks out all of Serena's clothes and—while Serena says she likes that her mom pays for some expensive pieces—you can tell Serena is kind of lost. She's dressed up like someone else and doesn't know who she is.

Besides that, her mom makes recommendations on what Serena should do and who she should do it with. Her mom has a controlling personality, so Serena doesn't argue with her. I guess she knows it's pointless, but I can see in Serena's eyes that her life is not much fun. She seems depressed and kind of dead inside. I think she secretly despises her mom. It's sad. I asked her once if she ever tried to talk to her mom about all these intrusions into her life. Serena just laughed a sad little laugh. I feel sorry for her. I guess I even feel sorry for her mom. She's pathetic and lonely.

Get a Life

You need to get a life too, Mom. That may sound mean, but I'm exploring new territory, and I want you to do the same. When I was little, you had no freedom to pursue your interests because you were so busy being a mom. Life has changed now, Mom. I don't need you so much anymore. I need a little freedom, and so do you. Instead of focusing all your attention and energy on me and my life, why don't you go out and do something you enjoy? Pursue the interests you have had to sacrifice. I won't mind. Trust me: when you're happy, we're all happier.

I'm trying to become an adult, learning new things, forming opinions of my own, and exposing myself to what's going on in the world. What about you? Are you growing? Are you staying current with what's happening in the world? If you're not expanding your mind, what will we talk about when I'm a grownup too?

Don't Force It

So you're thinking that you do have a life and you do have your own interests. Do you wonder why I'm not more interested in some of them? It's because they are *your* interests, Mom, not mine. It's great that you volunteer in the church nursery or the soup kitchen, but when you try to force me to do the same, all I can think is, *No, thank you!*

Do you know why that is? Is it because I'm selfish? Is it because I don't care about others? No. It's because that's your thing, Mom, not mine. Even if I wanted to work in the nursery or help in the soup kitchen, it's hard to admit it when you're tugging on my arm and demanding, "Come on, you should do this."

In fact, the words "you should" make me want to turn and run. If I'm going to do something benevolent or generous or kind, it's going to have to come from a place deep inside me. Otherwise, it won't feel genuine. I think there's a Bible verse about giving gifts cheerfully. If I can't decide for myself that I'm going to, say, volunteer to read stories to children at the homeless shelter, then it's just no good.

If you want to encourage me to do something, don't tell me that I should. Don't force me with an agenda; just leave subtle hints. You could tear out a newspaper article about how the soup kitchen is short-handed, or you might mention that the church nursery likes it when young people help. Then leave it at that! Allow me the autonomy to make this choice for myself, and then, if I do, let me give from my heart.

My Future Is Not in Your Hands

I know you sort of believe this is true—not that you'd ever say these words aloud—but since I'm dependent on my parents for college funds, you think you should decide where I go to school and what classes I take. Maybe that's true, but the more you act like this is true, the more I will resist.

Case in point. Do you remember Madison's older sister, Morgan? She graduated from high school while Madison's parents were still married. They both insisted Morgan attend a college of their choice. Morgan wanted to go someplace else. She fought them on it for nearly a year before finally giving in. Well, Morgan spent the first two semesters partying and getting wasted. (Did I mention that this college wasn't exactly cheap?)

Why did she do this? Didn't she care about her future or her education? Well, Madison told me it was Morgan's way of showing her parents that they couldn't control her life. After she finally graduated (with an unimpressive GPA and a degree in business, which she didn't want), she couldn't find a good job. So guess what she's doing with that business degree. Next time you're at Starbucks, look behind the counter for the tall barista with the magenta hair. Yep, she's serving lattes and cappuccinos.

So instead of forcing a future on me—one you think is in my best interest—why not let me have a say in my future? In the long run, it could pay off.

When Others Are Watching

I know you care about appearances, Mom. You seem to care about your own appearance and mine, especially when your friends or family are watching.

It sometimes feels a little hypocritical to me. For instance, I may be wearing the same jeans and top you've seen me wear dozens of times, but suddenly it's not good enough. I mean, just because we're going to Aunt Sue's house for brunch (not that I had a say in this), you think I should spruce up. Naturally, I think I look just fine, thank you very much! That's when the confrontation begins.

Have you ever noticed that the more you seem to care about what other people think, the less I care? There could be a couple of reasons for this. First, you care enough for everyone else, so why should I care? Second, it hurts my feelings that you don't think I look nice.

Get serious, Mom. Do you think I want to dress like you? So the next time you're about to tell me that I'm dressed all wrong, why not think about it first? Ask yourself if it's going to be worth the battle, and if you think it is, why not try to avoid bloodshed by not saying something mean about my appearance? For instance, instead of saying, "That T-shirt makes you look like a slut," you could say, "How about wearing the T-shirt that brings out the color of your eyes?"

Finding My Own Talents

I'm sure I must have some natural abilities that are similar to yours. That's to be expected. Just don't expect me to admit it. In fact, in my need to separate myself from you, in my need for independence, I might deny gifts that feel too much like yours.

For instance, we both may love to cook, but do I want to compete with you? Do I want to look like a failure next to you? Do I want people to compare me to you? I don't think so. For that reason, I may not get serious about cooking until I'm in my twenties. You need to be patient.

While I pursue finding myself and my talents, I may show an interest in some things that are not my natural gifts. For instance, if I take up the flute and discover that I'm tone-deaf, I hope you won't hold it against me. If I take up drawing and I seem hopeless, don't offer suggestions or a critique. Just give me space and let me figure it out. Remember that we learn from our failures. It's better if I try something and blow it than if I never try at all.

I'll probably figure things out a lot sooner if you can keep yourself from intervening. My friend Zane thought he wanted to learn to play the guitar. His parents were supportive—they helped him get a guitar and lessons—but after a couple of years, he wasn't making much progress. Zane told me he was about to give it up when his dad made a negative comment about his musical ability. Zane dug in his heels and stuck with the guitar. While he admits that he's not the greatest guitar player and he doesn't even like it, he still plays sometimes—just to aggravate his parents.

Teens need to figure out these things for themselves. Help from parents can backfire. The best input you can give is simple encouragement and patience.

The You I Need to Know

If you think I'll be encouraged by hearing stories of how you or Dad did amazing things when you were my age, think again. Oh, I'm not saying I want to be in the dark about all that stuff, but hearing about your days of glory, whether true or exaggerated, could be discouraging to me.

I don't mind hearing about challenges you faced or times you fell flat on your face—then picked yourself up. I can relate to that. I can empathize with that part of you.

If anything, I have a tendency to think your life went smoothly when you were my age. I imagine that you never got a zit, that you were invited to every prom, and that your teachers all loved you. That's just the way my mind works, so if you want me to know you better, if you want me to relate to you, try showing me the side of

WAYS WE'RE ALIKE

* We have the same last name and the same relatives.
* Our DNA is similar.
* We're both trying to figure things out.
* We both think we're right most of the time.
* We both get angry and lose our tempers.
* We both have the ability to control our tempers.
* We're both hormonally challenged from time to time.
* We both have insecurities.
* We both try to cover up our insecurities.
* We both have a sense of humor—just not the same sense of humor!
* We both try not to compare ourselves to others.
* We both feel bad when we compare ourselves to others.
* We both have a love/hate relationship with ourselves and each other.

you that's not too impressive. Tell me about the time you were stood up or the time you got an F or the time everyone except you was asked to the prom. See how that impresses me.

Don't Compare Me to You

Fine, we might have the same nose, or maybe we wear the same shoe size, but I don't want to hear about it. If you tell someone we're alike in some area, I will probably vehemently deny it or try to change it.

Do you remember when you asked me why Madison bleached her hair blond? I think I answered, "Because she wanted to," but that wasn't the whole truth. Do you know the real reason she did it? It's because her grandmother told her that her hair looked exactly like her mom's when she was a teen. Consequently, Madison decided she hated her thick chestnut hair.

To be honest, I thought this was unfortunate because Madison's hair was beautiful. As a result of all the bleaching, she has to be careful because it breaks easily. On top of that, she has to shell out sixty bucks every month to get the dark roots touched up. All this because she didn't want to look like her mom.

Do you see what I'm saying here, Mom? Teenage girls want to separate themselves from their mothers. It's not that we hate you, exactly—although sometimes it feels that way. Maybe *hate* is simply the word we use for, "I don't understand you," or, "You make me frustrated," or, "You really hurt me."

Like I've already said, the time may come when I'll be okay with being compared to you. I might even take it as a compliment, but that time is not now, so if you see me doing something totally unlike what you would do, don't be offended. It's just me trying to figure out who I am. Oh, I probably won't bleach my hair blond, and I'm not planning to add any tattoos or piercings, but I do need to feel like I'm different from you—like I'm my own person. It would sure help if you would still like me.

When I Shock You

I admit it. Sometimes I like to shock you. All teens get a kick out of pulling the rug out from under their parents' feet. Why? Why not?

Okay, I know you don't think that's an acceptable answer, so I'll try to explain. For the most part, parents have all the control. They call the shots and have all the power. Can you blame us for wanting to upset the applecart from time to time? Maybe it's about power or control, or maybe it's just a rite of passage.

The way you react to shocking behavior can make or break the situation. For instance, if I tell you I skipped my afternoon classes to go to the park, how will you react? You could lose your temper and yell, "Why are you such an idiot? You know it's wrong to skip classes. I hope you get detention for this." But what kind of response will that evoke from me? I will go into hyperdefensive mode, and we'll soon be embroiled in a screaming contest.

On the other hand, you could ask yourself, *Why is she confessing this to me?* You could calmly invite me to explain why I thought it was okay to skip classes. Perhaps I'd say I was having a hard day, that someone had done something horrid or humiliating to me and I couldn't bear to be in school after it happened. You might feel a smidgen of empathy and invite me to tell you more. Perhaps we'd sit down and I would divulge that I'd been the victim of severe bullying.

So what if you had yelled at me and I had yelled back and stomped off to my room? You would never know what was really going on. Plus I would feel bullied at home, as well as at school.

In shocking you like that, I can gauge your reaction and decide whether it's safe to take the conversation to a deeper level—or maybe I just want to rock your world for no good reason. Being a mature adult, you wouldn't handle your own situations like this, so it's no wonder you don't get it when I do. Keep in mind that, although we are similar, we are also very different.

THIRTEEN

I NEED RULES

BUT THEY NEED TO MAKE SENSE

E ven though part of me wants to kick over fences, knock down walls, and break free of all restraints, I know I need boundaries and rules—just not stupid ones. To be honest, even if the rules aren't totally stupid, I still might break them. Being a teen, I will find excuses and rationalizations for breaking them, even when they make sense to me.

You might say, "Don't talk on your cell phone while driving," but I will hear, "It's okay to *listen* on your cell phone while driving." You may say, "Be home by ten," but I hear, "Be home at ten, then sneak out again at 10:15 and come back at midnight." You say, "Do your homework," but I hear, "Do your homework when you get around to it."

I realize I could be asking for trouble by being so honest, but I'm trying to help you understand how my brain works. Now you're thinking you should write everything down for me so there's no room to misunderstand your rules. Who has time to write or read a five-hundred-page document with every rule spelled out?

I'm just warning you that cut-and-dried rules don't work with me as well as they did when I was a kid, and I want you to under-stand why. You see, I'm constantly changing. My life and circum-stances are constantly changing. As I grow and mature, I want your rules to be adapted. I want you to trust me, to give me credit for having reasoning skills and the ability to make good decisions. Of course, I won't always succeed, but isn't learning to make good decisions our goal?

What's Your Goal?

Now, I have a question for you, Mom. What do you want to accomplish with your rules? I remember something I learned in chemistry or geometry or maybe both. There is a theory that you need to focus on your desired results to calculate the formula that will get you those results. So what is your ultimate goal, Mom? Let me list several possibilities.

- You want total control over me—robo-daughter, complete with a handy-dandy remote.
- You want me to learn self-control.
- You want to know where I am 24/7. Maybe you should have a tracking device surgically implanted in my neck.
- You want me to be responsible and make wise choices.
- You want to choose my friends and activities. You might want to enlist me in the geek club.
- You want me to make good friends and develop strong social skills.
- You want me to do my homework so I don't flunk out of high school and humiliate you.
- You want me to use my study time wisely and to care about my grades.

- You want my room to be clean, so you won't be embarrassed when one of your friends peeks in my door (which they should never do!).
- You want me to keep my things in order so I can function.
- You want me to do household chores so you won't have to.
- You want me to help out around the house because it's the right thing to do.
- You want me to obey curfew so you won't have to worry about me.
- You want me to care enough about my family to come home on time.

Do you see where I'm going with this, Mom? If the outcome is to make you happy and to make your life easier, rules might not work so well; that is, if you set rules that focus only on keeping you in your comfort zone, I'm likely to rebel. Fair warning.

Negotiations

So, what am I suggesting? Do I want you to throw out the rules and let me run wild? Well, yeah. *Duh.* I know that's not going to happen, though, so how about a compromise?

If you allow me to have a say in the rules, I am much more likely to abide by them. Okay, I can't guarantee this will be 100 percent effective. I can't promise I'll never break a rule that I helped to establish. Get real. But it's a lot better than my digging in my heels and deciding to buck the system and break every single rule you make, just because I can.

So, instead of writing out a five-page contract describing your expectations for my behavior, why not sit down with me and have a real conversation? (Okay, do not attempt this while we're in the midst of a heated argument about my coming home after curfew. If you're smart, you will save this discussion until morning.)

When we sit down to discuss what kind of rules will be most helpful, make a point of listening to me, because if I don't feel part of it and I'm not being heard, it'll be pointless. For instance, let's say you want a drop-dead curfew of 9:30 on school nights and I protest this rule. That aggravates you, and suddenly you launch into a lecture about why this particular rule is nonnegotiable, and I will either fight back or shut down. Then what will we have accomplished?

You need to let me express my opinion. For the most part, I may agree with your curfew, but I'd like to have some exceptions. "What exceptions?" you ask with your pencil ready, like you think I should be able to rattle them off. I can't. But what if I'm working on a school project at a friend's house and it's taking longer than expected? Or what if there's a weeknight event I need to attend and it doesn't end until ten? All I want is for you to cut me some slack. How about we have a curfew with exceptions? I could agree to get permission and to call you. Maybe we could both get our needs met.

KISS—or, Keep It Simple, Stupid

Too many complicated rules will probably go right over my head, not because I'm dumb, but because I don't want to waste precious brain space on a bunch of silly rules. Why not just keep it simple?

Your chances of getting me to cooperate with your rules will greatly improve if I can remember what they are. No, I'm not going to write them down on index cards and pull them out for quick reference.

Rule 23: Do not accept rides from strangers. You might think that sounds like a good rule, but I can think of several reasons I might need to break it. What if my car breaks down, my cell phone dies, and a bunch of thugs are approaching when a sweet little old lady pulls up and offers me a ride? I pull out index card 23, so I decline the ride. Yeah, that's going to happen.

So why not keep it simple? Why not give me credit for not being a complete idiot? I mean, if you've done your parenting job correctly, why wouldn't I use common sense? Okay, I'll admit I don't always use common sense, but I think it's in there somewhere. Maybe I'd be more likely to use it if I felt responsible for my choices and actions, rather than thinking you are the one pulling all the strings.

I know I can't tell you which rules to make, but I do recommend you keep it simple. If we both agree that these rules can be negotiated from time to time, your odds for success will increase, and we'll both be happier.

Selective Listening

You've accused me of being deaf. I, like most teens, have learned to practice selective listening. I tune in when I want to know what's going on, and I tune out when I don't. The same thing can occur with rules, especially rules I haven't been involved in making or rules that are too complicated and numerous.

Even if your rules are perfect, which isn't likely, I will still resort to selective listening. Like when I'm going out the door and you remind me of my curfew and say, "Have fun." Well, I am already aware of my curfew, so I tune that part out, but it's nice that you said, "Have fun," so I tune that in. Later that night, when it's getting close to my curfew, all I can remember is, "Have fun." So guess what? I do have fun, and I blow my curfew.

Does that mean you failed? Does that mean you should never say, "Have fun," as I'm leaving? Of course not. It just means that I'm being a typical teen, and you shouldn't take it personally when I blow it. I'm just thinking of myself, and it probably doesn't occur to me that you are worrying about whether I've been in a car wreck or abducted by aliens or smoking crack.

When I finally get home, I might use excuses like, "I forgot," or, "I lost track of time," or, "I wanted to call but my cell phone was dead." I'll say whatever I think will help me avoid consequences, because, as you know, I don't enjoy consequences. If I could have my way, there would be none, but you seem to think I'll learn from them. I suppose that's true, but you won't ever hear me admit it. It's not a fun way to learn, but maybe it's effective.

Consequences

So you're wondering what I'd recommend for consequences. I might suggest you send me to my room with a quart of Chunky Monkey ice cream and the latest DVD to hit the stands, but I doubt that would work. Would it?

Maybe we should negotiate the consequences for breaking the rules when we're making the rules. If I'm involved in this process, it'll probably make things simpler when it's time to dole out the consequences. Not that I'll be smiling and clapping my hands, but I might throw a smaller tantrum. Don't hold your breath, though. Remember, I'm a teen and teens love drama.

The thing is, if I agree to the consequences, there must be part of me that feels they are fair. Otherwise, I wouldn't have agreed, right? You can point this out to me (gently, please).

Perhaps consequences should also be negotiable. For instance, I'm out with Madison on a school night. We're doing some last minute shopping, because the prom is Saturday and her shoes are all

RULES I MIGHT ACTUALLY GET
(REMEMBER KISS?)

* Tell the truth. (I might consider this a goal more than a rule.)
* Respect my curfew.
* Obey the laws (now that covers a lot).
* Take care of my stuff.
* Do my best at school.
* Respect my parents. (Okay, this *sounds* good, but it won't be easy.)

wrong. We get carried away, and I realize I've blown my curfew. I try to call you but the phone is busy. When I get home, you ground me for a week (our pre-agreed consequence). I lose my temper because it's prom weekend. You insist that it doesn't matter, that I'm always getting away with murder, that it's high time you put your foot down, and that you don't like the guy who was taking me to the prom, so I can just forget it. Then you storm off to bed.

Well, that might not be such a good move, Mom. I understand that I'm acting like a total brat and you have a headache, but I do think that negotiations are appropriate in a case like this. Maybe my grounding could begin after the prom. Maybe I'd even agree to a two-week grounding (or not), but for you to put your foot down in an instance like this seems unfair to me. You would come across as a cruel and a mean-hearted prison warden. I might rebel. That could make both of us miserable.

Ask yourself once again what you're hoping to achieve from consequences. Is it to send me into a hysterical tailspin, where I make stupid choices because I'm so freaking mad at my tyrannical mother? Or are you trying to get me to learn something, to grow up, and to respect curfews and rules? If that's the case, we might need to talk after our tempers cool down.

Safe Boundaries

I know I need boundaries and that they're established for my own good, but most of the time I'm not consciously aware of this fact. As you may have noticed, I like to push boundaries and test the limits.

I'm just being a teen. I've probably been doing this most of my life. Isn't that how children grow up—by testing their limits? At first, I was confined to my crib, then I learned to crawl, then I stood up and walked. All these things help to expand my world. My guess is you cheered for me when I accomplished these things. I don't always hear you cheering for me now.

For instance (I seem to be stuck on this curfew thing), when I again come home almost an hour late, you're fed up. I'm feeling pretty good about myself and I'm about to tell you why, but as soon as I'm in the door, you let me have it. There's no negotiation, no discussion, no nothing. You simply shout, "You are grounded, young lady! Go straight to your room!"

Let's say I go straight to my room. I'm mad, so I don't tell you what happened tonight. Maybe I never tell you. Maybe I just bite the bullet and take my punishment, but the next time I go out with my friends, I'm still fuming at the injustice and don't make the wise decision I made on the night you grounded me.

Now you're curious. You're wondering what happened that night. Why *was* I late? Well, I went to a birthday party with Madison, and someone had snuck alcohol into the party. By the way, I was *not* drinking. Unfortunately, Madison was, and she had driven us to the party. At first, I considered calling you to pick me up, but I knew you and Dad were at the movies. I also knew that if I left Madison at the party, she might drive home under the influence, so I pressured Madison to leave the party. I made her let me drive, which wasn't that hard because she couldn't even walk straight. It took longer than I expected, because I had to pull over to let Madison hurl in the gutter. I thought about calling you, but I was driving and trying to obey the no-cell-phone-while-driving rule.

I finally got her home and helped her into the house. I was about to call you, but her mom popped in. I told her mom that Madison was sick and explained that I'd driven her home. I considered calling you as she drove me home, but I knew I'd have to explain why I was late while Madison's mom was listening. I was planning to tell you the truth (for a change), so I waited until I got home. You blew up, and I never got the chance.

I felt I was doing the right thing that night by helping my friend. I had actually been thinking about the fact that rules were made to protect us. I could see that Madison had broken the rules and might've tried to drive. Who knows what could've happened? I was feeling mature and grown-up and like I'd learned something. I wanted to tell you the truth and how I had a new appreciation for the rules.

So here's the challenge, Mom. I need you to help me understand and accept that good rules and boundaries are in my best interest. Believe it or not, you have the power to help me learn to respect my boundaries, but if you start beating me over the head with the rules and doling out consequences without hearing my side of the story, I might not ever get it.

FOURTEEN

I WANT TO KNOW ABOUT GUYS

NOT ABOUT YOU AND DAD

This is a touchy subject and one I don't care to bring up. For starters, I fear a question from me might result in a sex lecture from you, and worse, a lecture that includes details about your sex life with Dad. Oh, you don't think you're lecturing, but you should listen to your monologues. It also helps if your timing is right. Read the expression on my face. See if I am (1) embarrassed and uncomfortable, looking for a quick escape, or (2) tuned out, aggravated, and about to let you know it, or (3) acting aloof but listening. Unless you observe the third expression, you might as well give it up.

I am sending the subtle message that I've heard all this stuff before, thank you very much, or I can't believe you think I'm *that* skanky, thank you very much, or okay, maybe you do occasionally have something worth listening to.

Here's a suggestion, Mom. Do us both a favor and practice the art of nonchalance when I bring up a subject like boys or sex or dating. I might suspect your nonchalance to be just an act, but I'll probably appreciate the effort. When your eyebrows shoot up, or you make that weird choking laugh, or your eyes bug out, it makes me want to take back whatever it is I just said.

If you could just take a deep breath, pause to center yourself, and consider what I just said (or what I really meant to say) before you jump in with your maternal wisdom, I would be grateful. These moments are few and far between, and if you overreact, I will quit talking to you.

Think about it. I have lots of friends who claim to know all there is to know on these subjects, and many of them are eager to share their expertise. The problem is, I'm not always sure about the accuracy of their stories and facts. Some of my friends tend to exaggerate, and certain girls love to set up other girls to make total fools of themselves, especially when it comes to boys, sex, and dating. When you get the chance to talk to me, don't blow it.

Jumping to Conclusions

Here's another heads-up, Mom. Don't jump to conclusions. For instance, if I casually tell you that I'm thinking about taking birth control pills, don't automatically respond with, "No way!" and launch into a lecture about why premarital sex is wrong, listing every bad thing that could happen to me, from losing my self-esteem, to pregnancy, to genital warts. That's just TMI (as in too much information). Naturally, I would be so disgusted that I'd storm off to my room and slam the door.

If this happened, you'd probably stand there in the kitchen, certain that I am either having sex or planning to have sex. You'd freak over whether I might be pregnant or if I've contracted an STD or whether you should allow me to see a boy again.

What if I were asking about the pill because Madison said it clears up acne, and I've been seriously breaking out? What if I have no intention of having sex until my wedding night? Do you know how I feel when you assume I'm already having sex or even seriously thinking about it? Guess what? When you think the worst of me, I want to live up to your low expectations. How does it make you feel when someone thinks the worst of you?

Listen to what happened to Madison. She had just started going out with Cooper when Madison's mom decided that they were having sex. Okay, I guess it's because she caught them in Madison's bedroom, but Madison swore they were just listening to music and kissing. That was it.

Madison's mom gave her this big lecture about safe sex, then she made an appointment with her gynecologist. Madison was pretty ticked but went along with it. The doctor, with her mom's encouragement, gave Madison a prescription for birth control pills. At first Madison was offended, but she got over it and decided it was pretty funny. She put the cool little pill container in her purse and showed it off to her girlfriends, like she was quite the grown-up woman. To be honest, I'm not sure if Madison is really having sex now. I'm not even sure I want to know, but the thing is, her mom practically pushed her into it. How weird is that?

Don't jump to conclusions, Mom. If I ask you about birth control pills, I might simply be thinking about my complexion. On the other hand, I might be thinking about sex. The point is to listen to me so you'll really know what's going on in my head.

Conversation Killers

Speaking of jumping to conclusions, there's something else that will shut me down. Admittedly, it doesn't take much to shut me down when the subject is as dicey as sex, boys, and dating. I guess you could say that you're already skating on thin ice, so you might want to keep your cliché one-liners to yourself. Here's a short list of things to watch out for.

- "Nice girls don't do that."
- "Teenage boys only think about sex."
- "Don't do anything I wouldn't do."
- "It's impossible to just be friends with a teenage boy."
- "If you look like a slut, boys will treat you like a slut."
- "If you have sex, you'll get pregnant."
- "Just because other kids are doing it, doesn't mean you should."
- "You're not going out of the house wearing that!"
- "I know you'd never do something like that."

Third-Person Observations

The truth is, I am curious about sex, and I have ways of collecting information. I'm just not sure that my sources are totally accurate. Here's a way you might be able to help, Mom. For instance, we're watching a TV show, let's say it's a rerun of *Sex and the City*—which you say you hate, though I suspect you sort of like it. As we're watching it together, you make casual observations about the characters. (I don't mean harsh judgments, because that's a real shutdown.) It's obvious that Samantha is about to go to bed with a guy she hardly knows. You might casually say, "I wonder how Samantha will feel the next morning, when she realizes they're not even in love." Okay, I know you'd rather launch into a big lecture about how premarital sex destroys a person's soul, but take it easy, Mom. Just make a casual observation, and see how I respond. If I respond, maybe we'll have a conversation—not a lecture or a monologue from you about how sex outside of marriage is a big mistake, but a real conversation where I actually consider something deeper than just abstinence for the sake of abstinence. It could happen.

The thing is, if we're talking about a character like poor, confused

THINGS I DON'T GET ABOUT GUYS

* Why do they act tough yet get their feelings hurt?
* Why aren't they more sensitive to our feelings?
* Why do they tease us?
* Do guys really think about sex 24/7?
* Why are guys so physical about everything—like pushing and shoving?
* Why do some guys lose their tempers so easily?
* Why aren't guys better at communicating their emotions?
* Why do guys like hanging with a bunch of other guys?
* Why are they so possessive at times?
* Why do they get jealous or angry? And is that okay?
* Why do I sometimes like the wrong guys?
* How do I make the right guy notice me?
* Why do guys dump girls and break their hearts?
* Will I ever find a guy who will treat me right?

Samantha (or maybe someone in a movie, or a character in a book, or even a real celebrity who's making some dumb choice), we're in a safety zone. We're talking about someone else, in third person. Not you. Not me. And not one of my friends, who I might be quick to defend.

It's a lot easier for me to take in information and hear your opinions on morals and values when we're casually talking about someone else. It's like we've set our own emotional baggage aside, but as soon as you turn that camera lens back on me or point your finger at me, I just want to get out of there. The conversation is over.

Image Issues

I know my clothing and general appearance are always high on your complaint list, Mom. I get particularly aggravated when you act like I'm dressing to attract attention from guys. That is so lame. Don't you know that most girls dress to impress other girls? Maybe we're enslaved to fashion, but that's normal. To assume I'm wearing certain items of clothing just to turn on a guy is totally bogus. Do I mind if my outfit makes a guy look twice? Probably not, but that's not my main goal, okay?

Here's another news flash, Mom: dressing this adolescent body is a new thing for me. I mean, I haven't had these boobs and this figure for very long. Excuse me if I don't always get my clothes right—according to you, that is.

If you think I need help in this area—and, okay, maybe I do—you ought to work on your approach. For instance, "Don't you know what kind of sexual messages you're sending to boys when you wear that skimpy top?" is not going to help. If anything, it'll make me mad, and I'll be more determined than ever to wear that skimpy top. Instead, gently guide me to a different top, perhaps by using a compliment. Tell me how the color really makes my complexion look pretty, or tell me that the neckline makes my neck look slender. Whatever. Just don't be negative. I constantly rag on my own appearance and don't need any more negative input.

If you handle these things well and learn how to be positive and encouraging, keeping your hasty judgments about my appearance to yourself, maybe I'll sometimes want your help with clothes. You can gently guide me toward styles that are cool without being skanky, and then we'll both be happier. Hey, it could happen.

Silent Treatment

I know that some parents are uncomfortable talking to their teens about sex. They shove a sex book at their teens and say, "Read it, and let me know if you have any questions." That might work for some teens, but I doubt it. It's like saying you really don't want to talk about it, and that's a huge mistake. Silence is easy to misinterpret. I will assume your silence means, "Figure these things out for yourself," or, "Whatever you do is okay, just don't tell me about it." I can also take your silence as a hint that you have sexual hang-ups, and that can feel confusing to me. I wonder why you would have these inhibitions and if I will wind up like you. That's scary.

What if something happens to me, and I really need to talk to you? You've already sent me a clear message that we don't talk about sex. Period. So I don't tell you I was the victim of date rape last night. I just stuff the pain down inside and feel guilty and dirty and ashamed, and I start acting out. You assume it's because I'm a teenage brat. You have no idea what's really going on, and I assume you don't want to know.

I know there's a fine line between making a pest of yourself and slamming the doors on communication, but I need to know that you are approachable, that you will listen to me. I need to know that you won't lecture me or judge me if I bring up a tough subject. When it comes to questions about sex, silence is not golden. It might even be deadly.

Tough Questions

I might have some tough questions. I have my sources, but I'm not always sure they're trustworthy. Whether it's movies, TV, magazines, the Internet, or friends, I am getting a lot of information shoved at me. It's easy to get confused.

So how will you respond when I bring up a topic that makes you uneasy? Will you send me subtle hints by your freaked expression? Will you blast me with information and statistics? If you want me to come to you with the hard stuff, you need to be ready. For instance, how do you define sex, Mom? Some of my friends say that anything other than intercourse is not considered real sex. I'm not sure about that. Some of the things girls are doing with their boyfriends (and even casual guy friends) seem kind of freaky to me, not to mention skanky. It makes me uncomfortable to think about it. I'm sure it would make you uncomfortable too. How would you respond if I asked you about it? Would you freak and make faces and launch into some big lecture about what nice girls do or don't do?

What if I suddenly became worried that I might be a lesbian? Would that totally derail you? What if I told you that Madison and I were acting silly and trying to get attention at a party and kissed in front of everyone? Now kids are saying that we're lesbians. I feel embarrassed and confused, and I'm not sure that it's not true. What if it is true? Would you be ready for that conversation?

What if I think I'm in love with my boyfriend? I know he's in love with me. He says so all the time. What if he's pressuring me to have sex or various forms of sex? I feel torn because I want to wait until my wedding night, but I'm afraid I'll lose him. Would you be ready to hear about that? Would you be able to have a conversation that wouldn't shut me down and make me certain I will never, ever speak to you about something like this again?

I have tough questions. I'm just not sure that you can answer them. If you've failed at other forms of communication (topics we've already covered in this book), it's unlikely that I'll talk to you about heavy stuff again. I thought you should know.

FIFTEEN

I FIGHT BACK
TO REMIND MYSELF

MY OPINIONS COUNT!

Most parents assume that teens love conflict. You probably think I go around looking for a fight. I suppose that's sometimes true, but not always. At times I just want peace and quiet, but someone—sometimes you—starts something. There are other times I just want to put up my dukes and swing at anyone and everyone. To be perfectly honest, there are times I want to fight and argue just to be mean. I don't like that about myself, but sometimes I can't help it. It may simply be a symptom of hormones or the frustrations bubbling inside me. Do you think I'll ever outgrow that? If I were a shrink, I might have a better grasp on this.

You probably don't realize how insignificant I feel sometimes— okay, a lot of the time. It's partly my fault that you don't fully appreciate this, because, as I mentioned, I am becoming adept at covering up my feelings and insecurities. At least I think I am.

When I lash out and angrily disagree with you and act like I'm the expert on everything, you probably assume that it's because I'm a mixed-up, hormonal teen who's selfish and spoiled and full of herself. That's partially true, but sometimes I make these absurd and obnoxious statements and manufacture lots of noise and fuss just to reassure myself that I can. I get a sense of significance from it. Okay, it's kind of a twisted sense, but sometimes a girl can't be picky.

I know my opinions aren't completely founded and rock solid, but that doesn't stop me from spouting them, especially on the home front. To be honest, home is my testing ground. If I say it loud enough and frequently enough, it will become true, or I will finally hear myself and realize that I'm wrong. Even if that's the case, don't expect me to admit it.

Do You Still Love Me?

Here's the good news, Mom: when you hear me freely spewing my opinions at home, you can be assured that I feel relatively safe doing so. I realize you don't appreciate my tantrums, but I must feel confident that you won't send me to reform school or sell me on eBay.

I can't always be comfortable around my friends. I'd never admit it to you, but sometimes they make fun of me. The thing is, I'm trying to figure stuff out, and sometimes I do my best thinking out loud. That's just the way my mind works.

Someday I'll come up with better ways to express myself. In the meantime, I won't always hold back, because you've created an environment where it's safe for me to vent, an environment where I know I am loved and accepted for just being me.

Sometimes I Imitate You

Parents like to believe they're mature and able to keep their feelings under control. Then they have teenagers who show them otherwise. I've seen you lose it, Mom, and that always gives me the green light to lose it too.

We need to come up with better ways to communicate. Believe it or not, I follow your example—okay, not all the time and maybe not when you want me to, but trust me, eventually you rub off on me. If you don't like the way I'm acting, you might look in the mirror. I might be reflecting you. Maybe it's not you at the moment, but it was you last week.

HEALTHY WAYS YOU CAN HELP ME EXPRESS MYSELF

* Encourage me in an area of my natural talents.
* Help me acquire the tools to take my talent to a new level.
* Invite me to take lessons in an area of my interest.
* Put me in charge of something that shows you trust me.
* Encourage me to write my feelings in a journal.
* Challenge me to do something new.
* Allow me to redecorate my room.
* Let me fix a creative meal for the family without any help/criticism from you.
* Let me plan and take a trip (even if it's a small one).

The Price We Pay

When you lose your temper, you say mean things to me. I act like it doesn't hurt, but it cuts deep. Later, you'll apologize, and I'm supposed to forgive you and act like it's no big deal, but here's the deal, Mom: it takes a while to recover from those things. The words get planted inside me, take root, and begin to grow.

I'm not sure if my words hurt you as deeply as your words hurt me. I'd probably feel guilty if I thought they did. I just assume you have been around long enough to be able to sift through the crud that's tossed at you. I don't have that worked out yet.

We both pay a heavy price when our anger flies out of control, and we shoot mean words like arrows at each other. Those arrows are landing inside me. Maybe you can show me how my words are hurting you—not by telling me what a mean, nasty, horrid person I am, but by simply saying, "What you just said to me hurts."

I might not quit saying mean things. I might not even say I'm sorry. I might think about it, though, and I might tell you how your words hurt me. Then we might call a truce and take separate time-outs until we calm down.

I Need Respect Too

You say, "Respect is a two-way street." Well, I need respect too, Mom. When I feel respected and listened to, I act differently. Try it sometime if you don't believe me. When you treat me like an adult, when you ask for my opinion or ask me for help with something, or when you pause to listen to something I feel passionate about and don't judge me, I stand a little taller. I feel a little older. I treat you with more respect too. I guess respect begets respect.

New Forms of Expression

I'm sure there must be better ways for me to feel significant, validated, and listened to than fussing and shouting, but it would help if you encouraged me toward them.

You might start by reminding me of something I'm good at and how I can use a natural talent to relieve stress and to express myself. If I show talent in art, why not encourage me to create something as a form of expression? If I'm a good writer, why not buy me a cool journal and pen and suggest I describe my feelings on paper,

HOW DO YOU SPELL RESPECT?

R = Reasonable

E = Encouraging

S = Self-controlled

P = Patient

E = Empathetic

C = Compassionate

T = Trustworthy

promising me you won't invade my privacy and read it? If I like design, why not empower me to redecorate my room, allowing me to make all the decisions? Whether it's sports or dance or fashion or music or poetry or basket weaving or whatever, why not encourage me in my areas of gifting and see if I begin to feel better about myself?

Be careful to not get overly involved, though. Other than helping with supplies and lessons, you need to take a step back, keep quiet, and take a hands-off approach. The last thing I need is for you to direct me, even if you are the expert. You need to let me do it myself—to make a mess of it, if necessary. When you step in and attempt to help—unless I beg you—I start to feel insignificant and want to give up.

Your job will be that of bystander and occasional cheerleader. (Just don't go overboard on the cheering.) Keep your criticism to yourself, even if I ask you! If you say anything that smacks of negativity, I will probably take it wrong. If you say, "Why not add a cloud to that skyscape?" I will hear, "You're doing it all wrong," or, "You're such a failure," or, "Too bad you're not as talented as (fill in the blank)."

If you can't say something positive, keep your thoughts to yourself and simply nod or smile and say, "Oh, my," as if you're impressed. Even if I design a dress that's held together with duct tape and safety pins, it's my creation—my expression—and it's a part of me. If you dis it, you dis me. My taste is not your taste. The way I do things is not the way you do things. That's the point. I am expressing me—not you. Just let me be me.

I may someday do things that are more to your liking. In the meantime, if your goal is to help me become more confident and competent and to feel significant enough to quit acting like a bratty teenager who throws I-need-attention temper tantrums, you might want to give me moral support.

SIXTEEN

I'M AFRAID

SOMETIMES

I try to act like nothing worries me, like I'm not afraid of anything. Sometimes that's exactly how I feel. At other times, though, I feel frightened—not by things that go bump in the night, although I still get spooked like that too. I'm talking about bigger things, and since this book is about confessions, I'll admit to some of the things that freak me out. Please don't hold these things against me.

It's not easy to confess that I worry about what I would do if something happened to you, but I do. Not on a daily basis, but once in a while it hits me how much I need my parents and my family. I would be lost without you. I'm sure parents don't think their teens worry about things like death or divorce, but most of us do.

When Marissa's mom died from cancer last year, I spent a few sleepless nights, worrying that it could happen to me. What would I do if I lost you or Dad like that? You probably didn't notice, but I treated you a little better for a while after that. Okay, it didn't last long, but I'm a teen. What can I say?

I don't just worry about losing someone I love. I know I act like I think I'm immortal at times (especially when I do something stupid and dangerous), but sometimes it hits me that I could die too. When those kids rolled an SUV last summer, I saw their pictures on the news and realized that they were the same age as me. That hit me hard. I just sat there and thought, *Wow! That could happen to me.* I felt afraid to ride in a car.

Oh, I knew it was ridiculous, and I wouldn't have admitted my crazy phobia to anyone—not even my closest friends—but I feared I would be next, that it would be my photo on the news and my friends looking at it, shaking their heads.

Sometimes I wake up in the middle of the night and wonder what it would feel like to be dead. It's a frightening thing to consider. I do believe in God and heaven, but it's frightening to imagine being dead. It scares me. I feel silly saying this out loud, especially in the light of day.

The hard part is, I don't know how to handle terror like that in the wee hours of the morning. I try to pray, and that helps a lot, but sometimes I want someone to talk to, someone who won't make fun of me or make light of my fear. I wonder if you ever feel like that too, Mom, and if this is something I will eventually outgrow. I probably won't ask you about it, though. It's hard to admit to having unsubstantiated fears. It makes me look weak and childish. You know I don't like that.

When the timing seems right, I might be open to hearing how you deal with your fears, if you have any. Do you ever think about death or what it feels like to lose someone you love? Just remember, Mom, timing is everything.

The World at Large

There are other things that worry me too. Some aren't quite as difficult to talk about, although I don't like to admit that these things scare me. I worry about global warming and environmental concerns. Okay, I know that probably sounds dumb, and you probably never give these things a second thought. Or do you?

I read and hear things that are pretty scary. I'm afraid the planet is going to fall apart before I get a chance to grow up or do some fun things or get married. Who knows, I might even want to have kids. I mean, is that too much to hope for?

I watch documentaries at school and wonder if we're all doomed. I try to remind myself that God is in control. I mean, if he created the earth, he surely knows what's up, right? Sometimes I don't feel certain, though, and some of the things I learn at school are not encouraging.

I don't like to talk about these things, because parents so often overreact, but these concerns trouble me. It's hard to imagine that the earth might be destroyed before I have a chance to experience life. You might not believe this, but that is one of the excuses teens use for having sex. They're afraid to wait, because who knows what's going to happen in the future? That sounds pretty lame, even to me. But hey, we're teens. We're not thinking like grownups.

When I think about my future and whether or not this world will be a good place to live, it's a little overwhelming and hopeless and even scary too. What about the wars in the Middle East? What about the terrorists who hate Americans? What about the countries with nuclear weapons? Do they care who they aim them at?

It's not like I obsess on these things 24/7. Mostly I try not to think about the madness around me, but sometimes I can't help myself. It worries me, and sometimes I need to talk about it. I try to talk to my friends about things like global warming and terrorism, but they say things that scare me even more. I don't think they know much more about this stuff than I do. In fact, they seem as hopeless and lost as I feel.

I need to talk to you about these things, but I don't want you to make light of my fears or tell me I'm blowing things out of proportion. I need sensitive and realistic answers, but more than that, I might need encouragement.

Local Fears

When I was little you didn't let me watch violent movies on TV. Although I protested, I was secretly relieved, because it actually was kinda scary. Now that I'm older, you probably assume that I'm mature enough to handle it. And I guess I am, but if I were totally honest, I'd have to admit that graphic pictures of violence still bother me. After seeing a particularly brutal scene, I feel uneasy and afraid. Oh, I don't show it. I mean, how juvenile would that be? I might even make light of it to cover up my true feelings.

Sometimes my imagination runs wild. Does that mean you should ban all brutal images from my sight? Probably not. That might make me sneak around and watch even more. I guess the best thing would be for me to learn what is or is not in my best interest. I need to evaluate what I'm watching and determine what's healthy for me.

Scary movies aren't the only problem. If I hear on the news about a crime that's close to home—like murder or rape—I tend to get scared. I sometimes wonder if I could be the next victim. This may seem unreasonable and unlikely, but that's just the way my mind works. I will pretend that I'm not the least bit concerned. I might even stay out after dark, despite your telling me not to, just to prove I'm not scared. I am, though.

I suppose I need gentle reassurance, but not in a babying way. It won't help if you get all paranoid and phobic about this stuff, because I'll either become more fearful and paralyzed, or I'll try to act like I'm not. Mostly I just need you to say intelligent and encouraging things, without belittling my fears.

If you have tips on how I can escape my worry trap, I might be open to hearing them, especially if the timing is right or if I bring it up.

COMMON TEEN FEARS I'LL NEVER ADMIT

* death and what comes afterward
* doing something stupid in front of my friends
* losing a loved one
* being publicly humiliated or bullied
* being the victim of crime
* making a bad life decision
* global warming
* public speaking
* terrorism
* school shootings
* being friendless
* things that go bump in the night

I Scare Myself

Despite all claims otherwise, I know I'm human and flawed and weak. I am often afraid of the choices I make. I worry that a wrong decision might ruin my life. Ironically, that sometimes causes me to act reckless and crazy. I can't explain why. It's like my brain isn't working, or maybe I'm just trying to prove something.

There's a part of me that wants to rebel against even myself. Maybe I'm simply rebelling against the voice of reason in me. That can be scary, and I suppose it could be dangerous too. It's like I sometimes want to do the very thing I don't want to do. It's a dichotomy. I am complicated—a puzzle, a mystery—even to myself.

Anyway, I'm sure God has a plan for my life. If I'm paying close attention, I can sense him warning me not to do a certain thing. I don't always want to listen. I would rather push the envelope. That scares me.

That's why I need your reassurance at times. I need to be reminded that this is a temporary state of mind. Someday I might get beyond it. Okay, I don't want you to say exactly that, but I do need your encouragement. I need you to believe in me. It will help if you remind me—quietly and gently—that I need to turn to God more often and that I need to ask for his help in making everyday decisions. Just don't lecture me about it.

My Future

Sometimes I'm afraid I'll never figure things out. It's enough to focus on getting through high school in one piece, but then I think about which college I'll choose to attend or if I even want to go. When I think about my future and the decisions I need to make, it's overwhelming. As a result, I usually try to push these troublesome thoughts from my mind, and if you start nagging me about them, I'll push them even further away. It's not that I don't care, even if I claim that's the case. I do care. It's just that it confuses me. I don't know how people make these huge decisions without uncertainties. Naturally, I want to appear confident and nonchalant, like it's no big deal. Underneath it all, I sometimes feel freaked.

There are a few ways you can help me. For one thing, whether I admit it or not, I do appreciate that you investigate the choices I'm considering. Okay, I do not want you to turn into an expert and tell me more than I want to know about a particular college, but it's reassuring to know that you're doing your homework. Just don't rub it in.

When it comes to actually making a decision, I want your input, but I want to feel like it's my choice. I need a sense of independence to empower me and give me confidence to choose the right path. If my parents step in and take over, I will feel insignificant, and that makes me indifferent. That is not a good way to begin the next phase of my life. In fact, that is scary.

Embarrassing Fears

Some fears are really hard to bring up. They may seem stupid, or I may not like to think about them. These are the kind of fears that someone like you might laugh at or dismiss. To me, they are very real.

For instance, what if I suddenly lost my friends? What if everyone decided that I was a total loser, and no one wanted to hang with me, and I became sad and pathetic and alone? What would I do? Maybe that's not going to happen, but there are kids like that out there. I doubt they go home and tell their parents about what's going on. I can't imagine how lonely that would be. I also think about college and how I'll be starting all over again without any friends. I could wind up with no friends at all. Do you know how freaky that feels?

Another thing I fear is making a fool of myself in front of my friends. When I have to speak in front of the class, I'm in the limelight. All eyes are on me, and everyone is just waiting for me to blow it. That is frightening. Even in a normal setting, I worry about looking stupid. What if my period starts and I don't know it, and I'm walking around school like that, and people are pointing at my backside and laughing? What if I have B.O. and everyone notices it except me? What if I wake up with a giant zit that is impossible to hide? What if I wake up with a bunch of them? What if my friends tease me behind my back because I've put on weight? The list could go on and on. You might think they're funny, but these are fears I deal with on a daily basis. No one will feel sorry for me for having them, but they are real just the same.

What can you do to help me? For starters, you can gently encourage me not to take life so seriously. Don't necessarily use those words, since that makes me want to scream. Maybe just tell me about a time you blew it and got embarrassed and how it turned out to be no big deal. Also, if you know I have something hard to do, like a presentation in front of the class, maybe you could be a little kinder to me that morning. A hug (not in front of my friends) would help, or just a pat on the back. It doesn't hurt to know that you're praying for me. You are, right?

SEVENTEEN

WHAT I NEED

MORE THAN ANYTHING

Okay, now it's time to get even more serious. Hopefully, you won't be shocked by this confession. Here's the deal, Mom. I *know* I need God as an integral part of my life. I know I need to be spiritually grounded. I know I need a solid foundation of faith and I need to live by my convictions. Will I talk about these things around the house? Will I make a public declaration of my spiritual beliefs at the breakfast table every morning? Will I live my life in such a way that everyone around me knows I belong to God and that I am faithfully obeying his will for my life? Don't count on it.

Once in a blue moon, I might mention my faith, but the sad truth is, I probably won't look like a believer nearly as often as you would like me to. For that matter, I probably won't look like a believer nearly as often as I would like to either. I sometimes take pride in my rebellious ways, but not in this area. I want God to be first in my life. I just don't always know how to make that happen. Sometimes it looks so impossible that I doubt I will ever get there, and it seems easier to just keep quiet about the whole thing. I mean, if I don't talk about it, maybe I won't be judged as harshly.

Here's my problem. If I talk too much about trying to live my life for God, you or someone else can throw it back in my face by pointing out that I act like a heathen at times. Okay, sometimes I do, but I want to change. I just don't know how to change. When I try to change, I blow it big time and things get worse. The harder I try, the messier it can become. At least that's how it feels.

Oh, I know that I should be learning from my mistakes. You'd think that I'd be a lot smarter by now. It doesn't feel very good to make mistakes when it comes to serving God. When I fail God, I feel like such a failure. It makes me want to give up. I wonder if I should take a spiritual break until I emerge from adolescence. I'm not saying I'd really do that, but sometimes I feel like it would be a lot easier.

I'm Conflicted

Speaking of easier, I wonder why it seemed so much easier to be a Christian when I was little. Even though I wasn't perfect, it seemed like I didn't blow it nearly as much. Faith came more easily to me. It felt natural, authentic, organic. It was a natural part of my life. It even felt like a comfort zone. I loved saying my prayers at night and going to Sunday school, but things changed as I grew older. Maybe I changed, because faith no longer feels like a comfort zone.

In fact, I feel like I'm living in a battle zone. I feel pulled in many different directions. My friends urge me to do one thing, my parents tell me to do something else, and that still, small voice gets drowned out. I get confused and lose spiritual equilibrium.

Sometimes I think I've almost got it under control. I make a good decision and feel somewhat confident, then the floor falls out from under me. I have a handle on how I'm going to deal with a certain challenge or temptation, but suddenly the rules or circumstances seem to change. For instance, this guy I've dreamed about suddenly asks me out, and during our date, he slips his hand up the back of my shirt. I get totally tongue-tied and don't know what to do.

My friends often create inner conflicts for me. I try to be loyal to them. I'm supposed to love them, right? But sometimes my friends want me to do things that I know are wrong. If I refuse to participate, they act like I'm being mean or selfish, and I feel torn. Okay, sometimes I want to do what they want me to do and I just pretend it's not wrong, which makes me feel even more torn and guilty and confused.

Compromised

Last semester, my friends and I were ticked at our history teacher because he kept surprising us with pop quizzes. He gave us no warning at all. He would just say, "Put away your books, class, and pull out a piece of paper." Then, wham bam, he'd hit us with a bunch of really hard questions. His only purpose, it seemed, was to ruin our GPAs and kill off any hope for academic scholarships. I'm not expecting any scholarships, but I have friends who depend on them.

One day, Cooper got a duplicate of the pop quiz questions from a buddy who'd been hit first period. Before history class, Cooper went online, printed out the answers, and shared them with some of us. Consequently, most of us aced the test, and Mr. Hemphill never figured it out. Okay, I felt guilty, but Madison said it wasn't really cheating, because old Hemphill was mean to surprise us with those stupid pop quizzes. Even so, I felt guilty, but here's the hard part: I wasn't really sorry because if I hadn't cheated, I would've taken a bad grade that day. Do you have any idea how much cheating goes on at school? Compared to most kids, I'm not so bad. Still, that doesn't make me feel very good about myself.

Convictions

Okay, I know it's wrong to drink alcohol, Mom. I've never had any intention of falling into this trap, but then I was with Madison and my friends at a party where someone had snuck in a keg. I usually try to avoid this kind of situation, but sometimes it's hard. I can't live in a cave by myself. Maybe I should have left the party, but it was at a respectable house, and the kid's parents go to our church, so I stayed and sipped on my soda.

Suddenly, Madison was angry because I wasn't drinking with her. She began to accuse me of being a bad friend. She told me I have a superiority complex. I guess you could call it peer pressure. I call it life as a teen.

I have to admit that sometimes when Madison pushes me, I don't know what to do. I don't want to make her mad. I need her to be my friend. Please don't tell me that I don't need friends like that, because it's not going to help. If anything, it will push me toward her and away from you.

It got tricky when Madison belittled me and said that I was acting like a baby. You know how I hate that. Still, I tried to be strong. I tried to stick with my convictions, but then another friend—a girl

I respect who attends our youth group—told me that it's okay to drink. She said that Jesus' first miracle was to turn water into wine, and that means it's okay to drink. At first, I didn't know how to respond to that. I pointed out that it's illegal for minors to drink. She said that in some countries it *is* okay—that the drinking age differs around the world and even in other states. I'm still not sure

WAYS TO ENCOURAGE MY SPIRITUAL LIFE

* Live your own best spiritual life.
* Stick to your spiritual convictions.
* Don't preach at me.
* Don't chastise me when I blow it.
* Don't nag me to go to youth group.
* Don't shove a Bible at me and tell me to read it as punishment.
* Continue inviting me (without guilt) to attend church with you.
* Encourage me to help those who are less fortunate.
* Keep me informed about things like youth group, camps, and Christian concerts. Just don't push.
* Don't judge me when I confess that I've blown it.
* Make wise choices that I respect.
* Lead by example.

about that. She said that if I was smarter and more experienced with other cultures, I would know that. I felt confused. I wasn't sure what I believed about underage drinking at that moment. Maybe I'm not even sure now. I do think it's wrong, and I know how you feel about it, but I can still get confused.

To make matters worse, some kids from school have parties where alcohol is served to minors and the parents actually know about it and encourage it. They actually provide the alcohol and say that it's better than letting kids sneak around and get into trouble. They brag that they don't allow the kids to drive home drunk. I suppose that's responsible, but it still seems weird that parents are handing out drinks to kids, as if it's okay. The kids seem to feel that it's okay, so it can be confusing. Instead of being a black-and-white issue, it feels kind of gray and murky to me. Can you understand where I'm coming from on this?

Okay, I can see you winding up for a big lecture about now. Trust me, I already know how you feel about underage drinking, but here's the deal, Mom: I don't want to base my decisions on my parents' convictions. I want to form convictions of my own. I want to know what I believe and stand firmly by my beliefs. It's just not always that easy or obvious.

Relationship

I know I need a more intimate personal relationship with God. Sometimes I think I'm getting closer to that; at other times, I think I'm totally lost and will never figure it out. I watch other kids who seem to have it all together. They seem to have all the answers and will probably grow up to be preachers or missionaries or something amazing. On the other hand, some Christian kids are as messed up as I am. One girl in my youth group, who always preached to everyone about abstinence, got pregnant. Go figure.

In the midst of my spiritual maze, it helps to know that my family is trying to live for God. Even though I complain about being dragged to church, I'm thankful you go to the trouble. My reluctance is because I'm lazy and like to sleep in. I know that's selfish and immature, but that's where I am sometimes.

There are things I can do that will help me learn to depend on God. I can develop good habits, but I will need some encouragement (not nagging) in these areas, and it might take time.

My Own Journey

I'm beginning to realize that this is my spiritual journey, Mom. It's not yours. It's a journey that I will have to walk alone. I have my Christian friends and my church and my family to back me up, but when it comes to making decisions for God and sticking with them, it's up to me. While that's a lot of pressure, it's kind of freeing. I have some control over my life. Whether I make good choices or fall flat on my face is up to me, right? I suppose that reality makes me want to try harder to do the right thing. The fact that I can't expect you to do this for me makes me feel more grown-up.

As hard as it might be for you to let go, Mom, it's probably what you need to do. You may not be able to do it all at once. You have a better grasp on this than I do, but you need to respect that it's my spiritual journey, even if I make a few wrong turns and fall down about a million times. Hopefully, I'll figure it out and get there in the end.

I might occasionally like a word of advice or encouragement or a gentle reminder, but the most powerful thing you can do for me—even more so as I get older—is to pray for me. I don't think we can overestimate the power of prayer. There's a Bible verse that tells us to pray instead of worrying about things. I'm sure you feel like worrying most of the time, and I'm sure I give you lots of opportunities to worry, but why not pray for me instead? I have a feeling it'll be better for both of us.

EIGHTEEN

LAST WORDS

BECAUSE YOU KNEW I'D GET THE LAST WORD, RIGHT?

Wow, Mom. I can't believe you made it to the end of this book—or did you sneak ahead to see what's in the last chapter? In that case, you've missed out. Okay, I'll give you the benefit of the doubt and believe you actually read or at least skimmed the book. That means you love me, right? Maybe you really do want to understand me. Maybe you really want to improve our relationship.

I wonder if you feel smarter or irritated or just confused by the experience. Maybe all three. If that's the case, join the club. It's not easy being a teen. Perhaps this book has been a good reminder of that to both of us.

I also know it's not easy being the parent of a teenage girl. I realize that it's a thankless job…and sometimes worse. And I kind of doubt that God will give you any special rewards for your bravery. I'm guessing there aren't any medals of valor for parents of teens, but I hope you'll experience moments here and there that might feel like a reward.

One of those moments may be when you catch me making a choice that makes you proud. Maybe it'll be declining to go out with "friends" when I know it could turn out badly. Or perhaps it'll be a time when I tell the truth and pay the price for it later. Or I might simply clean up the kitchen without being asked or nagged. Or maybe you'll observe me being understanding to a friend who doesn't really deserve it. Who knows, you might even catch me reading my Bible or praying—it's possible. Maybe you'll discover that, instead of sleeping in, I'm actually volunteering at the soup kitchen on a Saturday morning.

Because despite how I act at times, I hope that I will make you proud of me…someday. Whether it's bringing home a good report card or graduating from high school, I hope there will be something that makes you feel that your time and sacrifice were worthwhile. I realize it could take time, but I hope that eventually you'll get some kind of a payoff.

Like someday I could end up looking like the young woman you've always hoped I might, and—hey, who knows? I might even begin to dress in a way that doesn't embarrass you when we're out in public. And I might even decide to go to your alma mater after all, and I might graduate with honors…or not…because I know you'd still love me anyway. And maybe, when I'm much older, I'll bring home a great guy who you'll think is amazing and wonderful and mature. And maybe I'll think he is too. Or perhaps I'll decide to roll up my sleeves and become a missionary in Uganda and spend my life serving God and AIDs orphans. It could happen.

Or maybe I'll want to be like you and get married and have children, which would turn you into a *grandmother*! What would you think of that, Mom? And if that ever does happen (like twenty years from now), I know I'll need you more than ever. And I know that you'll be there for me. Because you've always been there for me,

Mom. And I really do appreciate that. And that's why I want to take some time to thank you.

I want you to know that, despite rarely saying these things out loud, I really do appreciate you. I will never become the woman I need to be (or the woman you want me to be) without your love and support and encouragement. And so I want to take time to really thank you, Mom. Here is my final list.

- Thank you for trying to improve your parental skills.
- Thank you for caring about my life.
- Thank you for not giving up on me.
- Thank you for being patient—even when I don't deserve it.
- Thank you for trusting me—sometimes.
- Thank you for keeping an eye on me—without being too obvious.
- Thank you for controlling your anger—even when I'm pushing your buttons.
- Thank you for believing in me—even when I look like a mess.
- Thank you for expecting the best from me—even if it seems hopeless.
- Thank you for sticking with me for the long term.
- Thank you for loving me unconditionally.
- Thank you for being my mom.

And now I'd like to say that your work is done and everything is going to be just peachy from here on out. But get real, right? You know that I still have a long way to go. You know that I still need your help…just like I need your patience. And as much as I'd like to have it all together, I'm still just a teen. So don't hold your breath. And don't think that you won't need to go back and review all this great advice again from time to time. Because I get it: I know I have some growing to do—and I'm glad you're there, growing with me.

Thanks, Mom!

MELODY CARLSON is the award-winning author of more than two hundred books for adults, children, and teens, including *Finding Alice, Crystal Lies, On This Day, These Boots Weren't Made for Walking,* and the Notes from a Spinning Planet series. She is the mother of two grown sons and lives near the Cascade Mountains in central Oregon with her husband and a chocolate lab retriever. A full-time writer, Melody is also an avid gardener, biker, skier, and hiker.

Other Melody Carlson Books for You

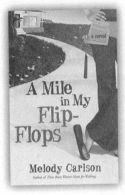

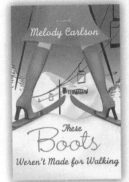

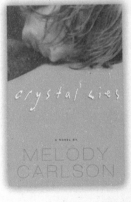

Melody Carlson Books

Diary of a Teenage Girl series

Samantha McGregor series

Notes from a Spinning Planet series

Available in bookstores and from online retailers